Putting Children First

A Volume in Honour of
Mia Kellmer Pringle

Edited by

Ian Vallender and Ken Fogelman

 The Falmer Press

(A member of the Taylor & Francis Group)
London, New York and Philadelphia

In association with the National Children's Bureau

UK   The Falmer Press, Falmer House, Barcombe, Lewes, East Sussex, BN8 5DL

USA   The Falmer Press, Taylor & Francis Inc., 242 Cherry Street, Philadelphia, PA 19106-1906

First published in 1987

British Library Cataloguing in Publication Data

Putting children first: a volume in honour of Mia Kellmer Pringle.
    1. Children — Care and hygiene
    I. Pringle, Mia Kellmer. II. Vallender, Ian. III. Fogelman, Ken
    362.7'95   RJ101

ISBN 1-85000-218-5
ISBN 1-85000-219-3 (Pbk.)

Library of Congress Cataloging-in-Publication Data

Putting children first
    Bibliography: p.
    Includes index.
    1. Child welfare. 2. Pringle, M. L. Kellmer (Mia Lilly Kellmer).
I. Pringle, M. L. Kellmer (Mia Lilly Kellmer). II. Vallender, Ian. III.
Fogelman, K. R. (Ken R.)
HV713.P87   1987   362.7   87-13649
ISBN 1-85000-218-5
ISBN 1-85000-219-3 (soft)

Jacket design by Caroline Archer

Typeset in 11/13 Bembo by
Alresford Typesetting & Design, New Farm Road, Alresford, Hants.

Printed and bound in Great Britain by
Redwood Burn Limited, Trowbridge, Wiltshire

Contents

Preface

Mia Pringle had already acquired a reputation for her academic rigour and communication skills when she was invited to become the founding Director of the National Children's Bureau in 1963. It was indeed these qualities which were seen to be essential for the creation and firm establishment of a unique multidisciplinary forum which would promote the interests of children. During her period as Director, from 1963–1981, Mia saw the Bureau achieve the status of a major research and development agency enjoying the confidence and support of central and local government, of academics, and of professionals working in a wide range of disciplines.

This acceptance by policy makers and practitioners is due in part to Mia's ability to communicate the findings of research through both the written and spoken word in such a way as to make them directly relevant. Many of the books and articles published during this time achieved a world-wide reputation. Her wide ranging contribution to the literature on aspects of child development and care can be seen in the complete bibliography included at the end of this volume.

This collection of papers, previously published in a variety of books and journals, aims to underline her breadth of knowledge of and concern for the needs of children in the light of research and practice. It serves to illustrate the very significant contribution she made to the development of policies at national and local level.

We are indebted to and acknowledge with thanks the many sources which have generously allowed us to reproduce these articles. Any profits from this book which accrue to the Bureau will be added to the Mia Kellmer Pringle Memorial Fund which was established to provide fellowships to support individuals to undertake study and writing on a particular aspect of children's needs or services; to set up inter-disciplinary seminars; or to analyse and report on some area of policy or practice.

Chapter 1

Are Parents Necessary?*

Necessary For What?

For learning to become human
Through his relationship, first with his mother, then the father and then an ever-widening circle of other people, the child is enabled to acquire a sense of personal identity; to model himself on the parent of the same sex and to understand the parent of the opposite sex; to make mutually rewarding relationships; to learn to walk, to talk, to reason — in short, to become human. The baby is born with this potentiality but it requires interaction with a human environment for its realization (*vide* the wolf children or Helen Keller). Available evidence suggests that it is through a stable, continuous, dependable and loving relationship with his parents, who enjoy a rewarding relationship with one another, that a child is enabled to develop his potentialities to the full.

To have unconditional, unpossessive parental care is every child's birthright. Just as malnutrition or starvation have damaging effects on physical development, so failure to provide adequate nurture for emotional, social and intellectual development will have detrimental, and, if severe enough, probably irreversible, effects.

Implicit in this concept of parenthood is the recognition that the child is a person in his own right — not a personal possession, as it were, over which exclusive rights can be exercised or through whom one's own possibly frustrated ambitions may be realized. It also implies an ungrudging acceptance of the constraints imposed on one's freedom of movement, time and finance.

What then are the responsibilities or obligations of parenthood? Basically, they are two-fold: first, to provide a loving, caring, dependable

---

*This paper was originally given at the National Children's Bureau's Annual Conference 1972, and published in *The Parental Role*, NCB 1972.

environment and to give this loving care irrespective of the child's sex, abilities, appearance or personality. Such acceptance is for better or for worse and is given without expectation of or demand for gratitude. The second prerequisite of good parenting is to allow, indeed to encourage, independence. This means permitting the child increasing freedom — of physical movement; of taste in food, play and clothes; and, perhaps most important of all, of choice of friends, studies, hobbies, career and eventually partner in marriage. Giving such independence does not mean withholding one's views, tastes and choices, or the reasons for them; nor does it mean opting out from participating and guiding the lives of our children; nor, indeed, condoning everything they may do. On the contrary, the young child needs a framework of guidance, of limits — knowing what is expected or permitted and what the rules are — together with the reasons and whether these are in his interests or in the interests of others.

This means that we must distinguish clearly between disapproval of their behaviour on the one hand, and on the other, disapproval or rejection of the child himself; and that the only lasting and really effective force for influencing their beliefs and behaviour is the model we ourselves provide: it is what we really are and how we behave which matters, not what we say or believe we are. By sharing our everyday lives, children learn about our values, standards, concerns and ambitions in a subtle yet influential way.

Sharing the parental role
Can such parental care be given in settings different from conventional family life as we know it? Communes have not been established long enough to assess their effects on child development. The Israeli Kibbutz is the only other Western child-rearing pattern which is markedly different. Upbringing is shared from the earliest months of life between parents and professional educators, the latter undertaking the major share of the daily care, training, teaching and disciplining.

Parental concern and involvement remain nevertheless paramount. Not only because the choice of the caring personnel, as well as the pattern of care, are decided by, and remain under the close surveillance of, the parents themselves; but also because each child spends three or more hours daily with his parents. During this time, they are free from all other responsibilities to devote their whole attention to playing with, talking to and enjoying their children. This is very different from the kind of half-attention given throughout the day in our society to preschool children by their mothers, busy with cleaning, shopping and cooking, and different, too, from maternal or paternal separation.

The type and amount of contact a child experiences with parents and contemporaries respectively, does, of course, affect his social, emotional and intellectual development. This has been shown in comparative studies of child-rearing methods — most recently in America and Russia — as well as by more closely controllable experiments with animals. The results suggest that Kibbutz upbringing may provide the best balance yet devised between the influence of peer group and of parents on children's personality development.

Yet much remains to be learned about how to assess the influence of environment and of relationships on child development; and about exactly how parental behaviour and expectations interact with the growing personality. Much more is known about the consequences of inadequate than of satisfactory parenting, most likely because 'happy families have no history' (Tolstoy). Parental disharmony and quarrelling, for example, are associated with anti-social and delinquent behaviour in children. The same is true where the home has been broken by separation, desertion or divorce. This is not usually so where one parent has died. The ill-effects of growing up in institutional care are also well-documented.

Parents, then, are necessary to ensure that children acquire maximal emotional stability which will make them resilient in coping with the inevitable stresses of life; and to foster the development of their intellectual and educational potentialities so that they may become fulfilled as individuals and effective later on as parents and citizens. What counts is the quality of personal relationships available during the most formative, early (i.e. preschool) period of the child's life.

Are 'Biological' Parents Always Better than Substitute Parents?

On this question, society's attitude in this country is ambivalent and contradictory. Both in law and in practice, we act as if the answer were 'yes'. Yet, on the one hand, we fail to provide sufficient community support to enable parents to look after their children in times of difficulty; for example, every year several thousand preschool children suffer the distress of coming into care because their mother is giving birth to another baby.

On the other hand, we so overvalue the child's ties with his natural family, that we allow him to remain with patently disturbed or rejecting parents. For example, a baby who has been battered is allowed to return to his home in the hope that social work support will avoid a recurrence, when both common sense and research have indicated that there is a high chance of it happening again.

To argue that the parent needs the baby for his own recovery is to sacrifice the child's welfare to that of the adult. Surely, it is quite unjustifiable to use a child as a therapeutic agent for his parents? To use a baby to 'cure' a mother or a marriage is exploitation at its worst. It follows then that it is as wrong to give a child to an adoptive mother merely because she can provide all physical comforts as it is to persuade a mother to keep her illegitimate baby merely because she has given birth to it; or to take a child back home who has been in care, when it has been necessary to stimulate the parents' faint and intermittent flicker of interest in him. It is over such children that one advocates a loss of parental rights. Their number is likely to be considerable since recent enquiries show that between a third and a half of the children in care at any one time have been apart from their families for five years or more; a proportion of these would undoubtedly be rarely, if ever, in touch with their parents.

Conversely, evidence has been accumulating in recent years which shows the powerful influence of 'good' (or 'bad') parenting. The most recent is our own study, *Growing Up Adopted*, while an American project showed that even older, rejected and ill-treated children are able to respond once they are placed permanently into the loving care of substitute parents.

Surely, society's view of the parental role is too adult-centred. Children are still 'victims without voices' whose neglect, ill-treatment, rejection or abuse come to light only in extreme cases. And when conflict arises between the rights of parents and the rights of their child, the resolution is usually in favour of the former. Undue importance continues to be attached to the blood tie. While it is being gradually accepted that a woman is not the property of her husband, we continue to assume that a child 'belongs' to and virtually is the property of its parents.

Yet it is evident that the willingness to undertake the responsibilities of parenthood are neither dependent, nor necessarily consequent upon, biological parenthood. Rather, it is the single-minded, unconditional desire, together with the emotional maturity, to provide a loving, caring home which is the hallmark of good parenting. Hence, should not the long-term welfare of the child become the first and paramount consideration? Of course, this raises the extremely difficult problem of determining 'unfitness to fulfil the parental role': by whom and on what criteria is that decision to be made? What safeguards and appeal machinery ought there to be?

Can One Parent Be 'As Good' As Two?

There is little doubt that one 'good' parent is better than two unsatisfactory ones, or than none at all. Nor is there any doubt that one-parent families, and particularly single-handed mothers, ought to be given adequate material and social support, if not for their own sake, then at least for that of their children. This we have argued at length in *Born Illegitimate*.

There is, however, currently much muddled and tendentious thinking about this question, which ignores psychological and even practical realities. It is epitomized by the glamorized picture of single-handed motherhood, proclaimed by ideological theorists and prominent, usually affluent, women.

Once it is accepted that the child's long-term welfare should be paramount and that responsible child-rearing is an arduous task rather than the conferment of exclusive ownership over another human being, then single-handed parenthood has little to recommend it, where there is a choice. Just to mention some of the inevitable social and psychological disadvantages in being brought up in a one-parent family: children need both a male and a female model with whom to identify; there tends to be an over-close emotional bond between the single-handed parent and her child; and the parent has to shoulder unaided the whole burden of caring, of decisions and of anxieties at periods of stress — all of which are more than halved if they can be shared with a partner.

The Way Ahead

I have argued that parents are necessary; that in Western countries no alternative and equally satisfactory mode of child-rearing has — as yet — been devised; that unwanted or rejected children are made the victims of our adherence to the myth of the blood tie; and that such children are likely to become the inadequate parents of tomorrow's children. In this way, we continue to pass on from one generation to the next the consequences of parental mistakes and disharmony.

To break through this vicious circle requires acting on, rather than continuing to pay lip service to, the principle that the long-term interests, development and well-being of the child should be the first and paramount consideration. If the key-note is to be prevention of future generations of inadequate parents, then some fairly drastic changes are needed in our national priorities. There are, of course, competing claims for scarce resources, for example, from the handicapped and the aged. But children are society's investment in the future. Moreover, the under-fourteens in the U.K. constitute twenty-four per cent and the retirement group only sixteen per cent of the total population.

Rather than arguing that we cannot afford to pay for early and comprehensive preventive services, I believe we cannot afford not to do so.

The quality of life is becoming a major issue of our time. Appropriate preparation and education of tomorrow's parents could hasten the day when society really cares for the children it chooses to have; who in turn will be mature and wise enough to accord the needs and the study of man the pride of place it deserves.

References

SEGLOW, J., PRINGLE, M.K. and WEDGE, P. (1972) *Growing Up Adopted* Slough, NFER.
CRELLIN, E., PRINGLE, M.K. and WEST, P. (1971) *Born Illegitimate* Slough, NFER.

Chapter 2

Young Children Need Full-Time Mothers*

The basis of my case is that homemaking, and the care of the young child in particular, are far too important, and too arduous to be considered a part-time occupation or, worse still, a spare time task. It is important, not only for the family itself, but for society as a whole. It is said that a country gets the government it deserves. I believe we also get the children and young people we deserve. The first years of life are vital for later development. Just as the foundations of a house are much more difficult to put right than if something is wrong with the roof, so the foundations for later behaviour, for relations with other people and for how we get on with ourselves, are laid down during the earliest months and years.

The case I am putting forward is based on three issues: first, on the needs of children during the first three years of life; secondly, that it is in the interest of the mother, too, to be a full-time homemaker during this period in her child's life; and thirdly, that it also makes economic sense, in view of the scarcity and high cost of high quality substitute care.

First, a word on our present attitude to the needs of children and why we should change it. We scrimp on the under-fives and on the young child, who is neglected, rejected or otherwise 'at risk' in his own home. This is false economy, because later we pay dearly for coping with emotionally damaged and delinquent young people, since by then we have no choice.

Where and why do we go wrong? Perhaps it is because we have never had a coherent policy for children. Instead, we proceed in a piecemeal, cheese-paring, uncoordinated fashion, responding to crises, doing too little and acting too late. Children do not suddenly become vandals, run away from home, commit suicide or murder. There are always early warning

*This is an adaptation of a contribution to the debate on whether young children need full-time mothers in the BBC2 *Controversy* programme, and was originally published in *The Listener*, 94, 2430, 30 October 1975, pp. 565–6.

signals that all is not well. Too often, these are heeded too late, when difficulties are longstanding, severe and multiple. All longterm studies of children confirm this.

The basis of a coherent policy for children is the promotion of responsible parenthood. This means that the parental life style is freely and deliberately chosen in the full realization of its demands, constraints, satisfactions and challenges. The need for young children to have full-time mothers is a vital part of this realization. The technical know-how is now available for the slogan 'every child a wanted child' to become a reality. Then there will be a much better chance that the needs of children are met. Two are of particular relevance in this context.

The first is the need for love and security. It is met by the child experiencing from birth onwards a stable, continuous, loving and mutually enjoyable relationship with his parents. The child's bond with his mother, then later his father, and, gradually, an ever-widening circle of other people is essential for developing his sense of individual identity and of being valued. This, in turn, forms the basis for all later relationships, both within and outside the family. On it depends the ability to respond to affection and eventually to become a loving, caring parent. Many studies here and abroad have confirmed that this is so.

The learning of self-control, and of moral values, is also facilitated by loving, consistent care. Full-time mothering is unique in the sense that the mother has the time, and hence the patience, to develop sensitivity to her baby; this enables her to recognize and adapt to his special, individual needs.

How important this full-time attention is has recently been summarized by Professor and Dr Newson: 'Dramatic evidence that babies and young children need mothering has shown that it is not only the mother's presence, but the rocking, cuddling and lap play . . . to deprive a baby of the natural expression of maternal warmth could prevent normal development of social relationships and permanently mar his personality'.

The less adequately a child's need for love and security is met, the more disastrous the consequences later on, both for the individual and society. Schools for the maladjusted, mental hospitals and prisons contain a high proportion of individuals who in childhood were unloved and rejected.

All the evidence shows that in Western society no adequate substitute has been found for the one-to-one, warm, continuous, loving and mutually enjoyable relationship which is the essence of maternal care. This is particularly so during the earliest years of life. However, that does not mean that the same person must provide uninterrupted care for 24 hours a day. Quite the reverse. It is wise to accustom even quite young babies to being looked after by someone else for short periods.

Love, though vital, is not enough by itself. The second need is for new experiences, which are as essential for the development of the mind as food is for the body.

The most vital ingredients for meeting it are play and language. Both take time and patience which the full-time mother is able to provide. Play is so important to the child because through it he learns to understand and cope with the world. Language helps in learning to think, to reason and also in making relationships. It is not merely how much talk there is but how rich the conversation.

It is very difficult to meet these needs by providing substitute care, since most available options have serious shortcomings. Even at best, they rarely provide adequate, consistent mothering or stimulating new experiences. Their most harmful impact is on the child's emotional and intellectual development. This, in turn, is likely to lead to educational difficulties once he starts school. Just as the basis for personal relationships is laid down in early childhood, so it is for scholastic progress.

Working mothers must seek some substitute care, but the choice available is limited. Many grandmothers go out to work themselves and trained nannies are beyond the pockets of most. The au pair girl lacks training and permanency, and often has an inadequate command of English. Other alternatives are day nurseries and crèches.

Such group care for babies and infants does not provide a high quality care either. Nor is it cheap. Estimated cost for 1975/6 is at least £15 a week per child, excluding capital charges.

Suitable staff are in short supply; poor pay and low public esteem militate against attracting high-quality personnel; the turnover rate is high so that a child may have a succession of young, immature nursery nurses or different child-minders; and the ratio of children to adults is high — usually five or more infants per adult. Another alternative is legally registered child-minding. While offering the advantage of a home-like setting, it, like day nurseries, has to meet good standards of physical care only. No such standards are prescribed for meeting emotional or intellectual needs.

Professor Rutter recently examined some 500 studies concerned with the effects of maternal deprivation. In the section 'Mothering in the child's own home' he has this to say: 'The quality and amount of maternal care provided in the average institution is much worse than the average family ... it does seem peculiarly difficult for an institution to provide parental care of the quality and quantity expected in a family setting.' The findings of my own work — both in research and directly with children — fully support this conclusion.

In short, only the very rich or the very lucky have access to satis-factory full-time, daily substitute care. To provide a high quality system would be very costly and take years to develop. In any case, is this really the best way ahead? Is not full-time mothering for young children a preferable choice and in the interest of mothers themselves?

Because of current social expectations, women are having the worst of all worlds. If they decide to have a career and not children. they have to withstand powerful social and family pressures. If they do what is expected and become mothers, then their contribution as homemaker with a young family is grossly undervalued. This is reflected in their complete financial dependence on their husband. Those who attempt to combine a family with work are made to feel guilty for leaving their children to be looked after by others, especially when the substitute care is unsatisfactory.

To cope adequately, a working mother has to be a 'superwoman': she needs inexhaustible energy as well as superb planning and organizing ability. To opt for a full-time job, in addition to the physically and mentally demanding one of caring for a young child, is to opt for the burden of hard labour.

Of course, I am not advocating that mothers should become second-class, dependent citizens, chained to kitchen and kids. On the contrary. Mothering should be recognized as the important, skilled, demanding and interesting job it is. Incidentally, it is the only one in our society which it is assumed everyone can undertake without either preparation or inclination.

Some argue that looking after a young family is a lonely and boring job. But surely the opposite is the case? Those who really like children and accept the crucial importance of the earliest years, find caring for them all the more rewarding. Observing their child's progress and fostering it bring joy and creative satisfaction. Surely working in a supermarket, factory or office is less creative and interesting? It is time we ceased to regard mother-ing as a dull, menial chore, wasteful of women's talents.

To meet the needs of women who wish to be full-time mothers for their own as well as their children's sake, two things are required: first, to increase the status of mothers by recognizing their unique contribution to the community. Secondly, to provide adequate financial reward. No mother of under-fives should have to go out to work for financial reasons.

How can we bring this about? Husbands should have to acknowledge the value of looking after a young family by sharing their income with their wives, as of right. In addition, the state should give substantial financial inducements to mothers of young children to care for them at home. In France, for example, this is done by means of a special salary which is paid to mothers, whether married or single. The amount is highest for those with infants under two years of age.

The finance required would not be wholly new. Considerable expenditure is at present devoted to day nurseries. More is being demanded.

These funds would be released if substitute group care were reduced to the barest minimum.

Also, full-time mothers should not be penalized once they are ready to re-enter the job market. On the contrary, having cared for their children should 'count' as relevant experience. Surely it would be an asset in many spheres of work, including teaching, social work, medicine, nursing and psychology.

Many women have been brainwashed to seek as a desirable way of life the heavy burden of two jobs — worker and homemaker. It is time to reverse the process and to recognize that young children need full-time mothers.

Chapter 3

Discussion Points on Low Cost Day Care*

The Four Aims of Provision for the Under-fives

To discuss low cost day provision for the under-fives confuses the issues involved because it ignores the fact that by now we have come to expect preschool care and education to fulfil four different tasks at one and the same time but for different children; namely to complement, supplement, compensate or be a substitute for parental care.

The first task, to complement the loving care and intellectual stimulation provided in the 'good' home, is quite circumscribed. It is required for the majority of young children whose mothers enjoy looking after them and where a few hours a week may be all that is needed or wanted. Its main aims are to make the transition from home to school less abrupt which is likely to aid the psychological weaning of both mother and child; and it provides the child with the experience of an emotionally less close but nevertheless continuing relationship with an adult while also learning to share her attention with other children.

The second task — to supplement — is required where there are some limitations or shortcomings in the child's environment. Among these are the conditions of urban living; insufficient space, in or out of doors, to accommodate large toys and equipment; lack of suitable playmates; or where the mother, for the sake of her own mental health, or for financial reasons, wishes to take up some part-time work outside the home.

Playgroups, one-o'clock clubs, kindergartens, nursery schools and classes are designed to complement and supplement parental care. In this context it makes sense to plan in terms of low cost expansion, particularly if existing buildings were to be brought into much fuller use, and maternal

*Sunningdale Conference Paper, published in *Low Cost Day Provision for the Under Fives*, published jointly by DHSS/DES, 1976.

13

participation became the rule.

The situation is, however, completely different with regard to the third and fourth tasks of preschool care and education. When parental care is inadequate to some extent or where the child has some special needs because of a handicap, then *the third task* comes into play, namely to compensate him for what he is lacking, otherwise he will be missing out on some aspects, vital to optimal emotional, social or intellectual development. Compensatory care and education aim to prevent the cumulative effects of early disadvantage or disability.

Despite the devoted efforts of those working with young children, existing types of preschool provision have so far proved largely ineffective in fulfilling this task. This is not surprising since none were designed to do so. It is this third role which is more in need of innovation and evaluation. Inevitably this means resources, not only in terms of manpower, training and research but in order to devise experimental schemes and special equipment. Hence it is unrealistic to think in terms of low cost provision.

The fourth task, to provide a substitute for parental care for the major part of the day can also not be done satisfactorily at a low cost. This is particularly so for the under-threes for whose optimal development a considerable amount of individual attention is essential. At present, child-minding is attempting to 'do it on the cheap' — the very term 'minding' devalues the importance of the job. The Scandinavian terms, 'family day care' and 'day mothers', are much more appropriate descriptions. These countries give more adequate remuneration as well as providing training, where necessary. A similar upgrading in status and pay in this country would contribute also to raising the general level of child care in the socially disadvantaged areas in which most childminders live. After all, they provide the same level of care for their own children which, in turn, does not differ much from that provided by most of the mothers whose children they look after.

That many women are willing to provide care in their own homes is witnessed by the many thousands of unregistered minders. Some training and better pay could greatly increase the quality of care which they provide. Even given these financial increases, family day care would still be less costly than providing group care in day nurseries. For practical purposes they are like residential institutions since infants and toddlers spend nearly their whole waking life there.

During recent years, research evidence has been accumulating to show that life in institutions has damaging effects on the inmates, be these adult prisoners, approved school or borstal boys, mental hospital patients or children in residential care or long stay hospitals. And the younger the 'inmate' the more harmful the consequences for emotional and intellectual development are likely to be. So at best institutions are not beneficial to deprived children; at worst, they can be deeply damaging. Yet it is the most costly form of care.

It is ironic that there should be such pressure in this country to increase provision for the group care of babies and infants, when countries such as Russia and Hungary who had promoted it on a large scale are now discouraging it. They had done so previously not only on economic but also on ideological grounds. Now they have come to consider that it has not proved to be an adequate substitute, either from the child's or the mother's point of view. Instead, a working mother receives substantial financial support for a period of up to three years for each infant so that she may stay at home to care for her young children. In France, too, similar encouragement is provided including a special salary which is highest for the under-twos. And might the image of maternal care not be raised by substituting for the term 'housewife' the more accurately descriptive one of 'homemaker'?

Guidelines to Good Practice

It would help to raise standards for the care of the under-fives, if central government were to issue guidelines in relation to emotional, social and intellectual needs. Because minimum requirements are laid down about acceptable physical standards, these may well be over-emphasized in comparison with the other aspects of children's development. Of course, such guidelines would have to differentiate between the needs of babies, infants, toddlers and the older preschool child.

Now that various innovatory schemes for the under-fives are being developed, it would also be conducive to spreading successful practice, if a descriptive list of them were to be prepared and made widely available. To be of maximum use, it would have to be updated every two years or so. This task could also be undertaken by central government but additionally it might commission a more detailed monitoring and evaluation on an ongoing basis.

A Strategy for the Under-fives

Matching Services to Needs

The present situation is socially divisive and paradoxical. It is divisive because a much higher proportion of children from middle class homes go to nursery schools and classes, whereas day nurseries and childminders are used mainly by poorer working-class mothers. It is paradoxical because a charge is made for the latter but not for the former. Playgroups cut across this division in that they make a charge but are used primarily by middle class mothers. It is rather puzzling that primary schools have for long been practically comprehensive and secondary education may soon become so for the majority, whereas preschool provision has remained quite rigidly stratified.

The ideal solution would be for all types of preschool provision to be available free of charge according to the child's needs and parental wishes. However, if for the time being the present economic situation makes this impossible, then would it not be fairer to make services free for those in need and charge the others, according to parental ability to pay? Though the means test has always been disliked, is this attitude not now becoming an anachronism? After all, everyone has to reveal their pay for income tax purposes and the parental contribution to be made for university students depends on parental income.

Prevention as the Key

In the past thirty years, many of the physical illnesses of childhood have been virtually eliminated, including tuberculosis, diphtheria and poliomyelitis. In the field of mental health, the picture is far less encouraging. Might not the strategy which proved so successful in improving physical health be appropriate also to other aspects of growth? The 'when' and 'how' of this strategy have, I believe, important lessons for the promotion of children's emotional, social and intellectual development.

Spectacular progress began to be made when the vital role of good preventive medicine came to be accepted. It was preceded by the recognition that the treatment of disease is a very inefficient way of ensuring good physical health. So it was decided to begin at the very beginning, namely with pregnant women and then their newborn babies. Similarly, available evidence indicates that it is very inefficient to rely on treating the school child who is linguistically retarded, educationally backward, socially inadequate and emotionally disturbed. Here also prevention is likely to be more effective. It too must start at the very beginning, from conception onwards, and continue throughout the child's earliest months and years of life. So much then for the 'when'.

Now to turn to the question of how prevention was accomplished. By providing maternity and child welfare clinics, by ensuring that pregnant women and then their children received the care and nourishment needed for proper growth, a virtual revolution was brought about within a generation. For example, fifty years ago, some eighty per cent of children in London's East End schools had signs of rickets and hence remained stunted in stature. Now the disease has almost been eliminated.

Child welfare clinics and the comprehensive preschool centres, mentioned earlier, would similarly be able to provide focal points for preventive mental health services. It might be argued that we do not yet have detailed enough knowledge about the causes of behavioural malfunctioning. Here again, the parallel with the physical field holds good. It proved possible to vaccinate and inoculate successfully against whooping cough or poliomyelitis without the understanding of why a particular child was more liable to contract the disease or how to cure it.

In the same way, there is now an understanding of the broad preventive measures which could raise the general level of children's intellectual, educational, social and emotional development. For example, there is evidence that mothers who are likely to abuse their baby can be detected even during pregnancy and hence counselling and supportive services could be brought into play then; conversely, the signs of emotional deprivation are apparent to the skilled, trained paediatrician or psychologist even in the case of very young infants.

Incentives for Seeking Preventive Care

For prevention to be successful, regular check-ups are essential and the younger the child the more frequent these need to be. The first three years of life are particularly vital, not only because development is most rapid then but also because irreparable damage can often be avoided during this period. For example, the amelioration of some handicaps, such as phenylketonuria or deafness, is most likely to be effective if commenced during the first few months of life; also it is the very youngest age group which is most liable to be abused and ill-treated.

In the case of preventive health care, the incentive for seeking it was not only its ready and universal availability but probably also the fact that subsidized baby food was obtained through child welfare clinics. Some might argue that the vast majority of parents have the well-being of their children at heart and therefore would also welcome a regular check-up on their emotional, social and intellectual development. There is a complementary argument which is that the state has a vested interest in such a preventive system since the cost of supporting and treating the backward, handicapped or emotionally damaged child is high.

An ideal incentive might be a special allowance for mothers who seek the required regular check-ups but again the present economic difficulties may preclude the introduction of such a new benefit. In fact, such a bonus system was used in France from 1945 until 1970; then it was decided that the sanction of loss of family allowances should be used instead. During the child's first year of life nine examinations are required; three during the second year; and then there is one examination every six months until the age of six years. A very high coverage, probably over 99 per cent, is expected.

If such a scheme were to be introduced in this country, it may be necessary to start with less frequent check-ups until enough trained personnel are available to carry out comprehensive developmental examinations. Some will argue that to operate sanctions against parents is an infringement of their liberty. As I see it, such legislation is, on the contrary, aimed to be helpful to parents in that it introduces at the earliest possible time not only supportive services but also diagnostic and treatment facilities as soon as the need for them is detected. Some may fear that children of poor parents will be penalized because they may be unable to take them for regular check-ups. However, there is no reason why these could not take place in their own homes or in day care facilities in which many of the most disadvantaged children are placed. Why is it assumed by the poverty lobby that poor parents are less concerned for their children's well-being than the more affluent? And why have French legislators found such a scheme acceptable to their electorate?

State intrusion into the privacy of family life should clearly not be advocated lightly. In this case, however, it has to be balanced against another major interest which must surely concern society, namely enforcing a child's right to care and protection, both of his physical and mental health. Should this not be seen as a basic human right? The state gives an allowance to parents precisely because it wishes to support good parenting and therefore it also has a duty to ensure that this is in fact being provided. For similar reasons, the state provides free education. The parent who refuses to send a child to school has to show — usually in the court of law — that he is substituting an acceptable alternative. In the same way, it would be open to a parent who refuses to have a regular check-up for his child to show that he is nevertheless giving adequate care. The family allowance would then be restored but only after the court had satisfied itself that the child's interests were indeed being safeguarded.

Universality versus Selectivity

As in the health field, it is highly likely to be more economical and effective to apply preventive measures 'across the board'. Then positive discrimination can be given to vulnerable families and to children who are 'at risk', whether because of home circumstances or because of a mental or physical disability. There are always indicators or early warning signs that all is not well with a child's development. Wherever possible, help should be given through and with the close involvement of the parents, especially the mother. As long as the care and educational facilities for the under-fives remain in short supply, they should be allocated according to needs discovered during the regular early check-ups. The Development Guides which have been devised by the Bureau for use by para-professionals and by parents could be employed as a screening device, as a source of additional information to aid a specialist examination and as a tool for teaching greater understanding of the growth and development of young children.

Additional References

BERFENSTAM, R. and OLSSON, I.W. (1973) *Early Child Care in Sweden*, Gordon and Breach.

FROMMER, E.A. and O'SHEA, G. (1973) 'Ante-natal identification of women liable to have problems in managing their infants', *British Journal of Psychiatry*, 123.

HERMAN, A. and KOMLOSI, S. (1972) *Early Child Care in Hungary*, Gordon and Breach.

JOBLING, M. (1976) *The Abused Child*, National Children's Bureau.

PRINGLE, M.K. (1971) *Deprivation and Education*, Longman in association with National Children's Bureau, 2nd ed.

RAPAPORT, C. and MARCUS, J. (1976) *Early Child Care in Israel*, Gordon and Breach.

SCHAFFER, H.R. (1971) *The Growth of Sociability*, Penguin.

SCHAFFER, H.R. (1974) 'Early social behaviour and the study of reciprocity', *Bulletin of the British Psychological Society*, 27.

WOOD, M. (1975) 'Cultural attitudes to child development', *Concern*, 18, National Children's Bureau.

WYNN, M. (1972) *Family Policy*, Penguin.

WYNN, M. and WYNN, A. (1974) *The Right of Every Child to Health Care*, Council for Children's Welfare.

Chapter 4

The Preschool Comprehensives*

The present climate of opinion has become much more favourable to the young child's needs than looked likely even twelve months ago. The preschool playgroup movement, nursery school provision, day care and preparation for parenthood have all become not only topical issues, but are now receiving government support and financial backing as well as a fairly high 'priority rating' in official thinking.

The changing pattern of family life, and of the role of women in particular, makes it likely that there will be continuing clamour for an increase in preschool provision. Also the gathering momentum of awareness that the youngest age group has hitherto been the most neglected, has now reached the stage where signposts to the most fruitful next initiatives can be discerned. These seem to point to three objectives: first, to the wider dissemination of knowledge about child development and the parental role; secondly, to the exploration of new forms of preschool care and education; and thirdly, to a greatly increased research effort into the earliest years of childhood.

Preparation for Parenthood

So far it is only in regard to the young child's physical development that our society has both accepted and acted on the precept that prevention is better than cure. Policy implications for health services have been thought through and, to a great extent, have already been translated into practice. In consequence the improvement — a virtual revolution — achieved in children's health and growth during a mere forty years is impressive. Certain diseases, such as tuberculosis, diphtheria and poliomyelitis, have been virtually eliminated. Physical maturity is reached earlier. And the nutritional needs of

*Originally published in *Where*, 81, 1973, pp. 165–7.

children are being so well met that obesity now rivals undernourishment as a cause for concern.

Now a similar understanding needs to be promoted of how emotional, social and intellectual development can be fostered. It must be made clear that maladjustment, intellectual retardation and learning difficulties are, in the majority of cases, not innate but related to lack of appropriate opportunities, to neglect and to deprivation; also, that even when a child has a disability, the extent to which this will prove to be a handicap and distort development will depend as much (if not more) on parental, and hence the child's own attitudes, as on the actual nature and severity of the disability.

An effective programme of preparation, rather than education, for parenthood would have to adopt a wide and comprehensive base. 'Education' is too narrow a connotation in this context, suggesting as it does classes and instruction, on the model of sex education. Also it conveys too formal a framework and too intellectual a conception, suggesting that 'knowing' is enough. What is required is neither a narrow course, seen as a branch of biology or home economics, nor a very wide and general one in citizenship. Equally it should not be confined, as it tends to be, to girls and the less intelligent ones at that.

Instead all schools should run a course in human relations and child development, with particular emphasis on what is now known about the importance of the earliest years of life for optimal physical, emotional and social growth. Some first-hand experience of very young children should form an integral part of such a course.

This first aim — of increasing the understanding and changing the feelings of future mothers and fathers — needs to be accompanied by a second: this is to bring about a change in the climate of public opinion, so as to influence in turn national priorities and official policy. At present home-making and motherhood are undervalued. It is ironic that the housewife with small children, whose working hours are often twice as long as that of the 35-hour a week clerk, is described as not being gainfully employed! Added to this is her economic dependence on her husband and her very limited legal rights in relation to her children, compared with those of the father. Little wonder that educated girls are made to feel they are wasting their ability if they are 'only a housewife and mother'.

Instead parenthood and the mothering of the very young child should be recognized as the extremely important, skilled and demanding job it is. Society ought to acknowledge the fact that children are its investment in the future by two measures:

First, a home responsibility allowance should be paid to any woman who devotes herself to the care of her children, so that there would be no economic need for her to seek outside employment. This should be paid to her as a matter of right, not charity, and irrespective of whether she is married or not.

Second, retraining facilities should be provided for women who wish to start employment once their children go to school.

Changing the Preschool Formula

Up to now the two strands of preschool provision — care and education — have developed and functioned separately. Day care is available for the young child whose own family cannot satisfactorily provide it, most often because the mother is either single-handed or for other reasons has to go out to work. Whether such care is given in a day nursery or by a child minder, the emphasis is essentially on physical aspects, though some opportunities may be provided both for mothering and for learning. Preschool education is essentially geared to learning, albeit in the wider sense of the term, though mothering and physical care do play a part. Preschool playgroups, being a self-help movement and hence largely middle-class, are nearer in outlook and scope of activities to nursery schools, except for their distinctive feature of active maternal involvement.

Rather than going ahead as planned with expanding these facilities in their present forms, we ought to question the theoretical as well as the practical justification for their separate existence. Might there not be positive advantages in integrating all the different types of provision into a unified system of preschool centres? The aim would be to minimize or eliminate the potential shortcomings, and pool the advantage of each type of provision.

What are these disadvantages and strengths? With regard to day nurseries (and very probably childminding, though evidence is lacking and we must wait for the results of Brian Jackson's Child Minding Research Unit), disadvantaged children — who may be already emotionally or intellectually neglected on admission — rarely receive either the amount of mothering or the stimulation which they need. Nor does the idea of providing 'special day nurseries' for the maladjusted or for the culturally deprived seem promising for a number of reasons. The advantage of day nurseries lies in the excellent physical care they provide and in the long hours they open.

The middle-class mother, who wishes or needs to go out to work, is more likely to engage some paid help to look after her young family. This has the advantage of not taking the children away from their own homes.

However since trained nannies are both too expensive and too scarce a commodity, *au pair* girls have become the most widely used alternative. This has several disadvantages. Many know very little English, at least to begin with. Most are themselves young and may have little understanding of a small child's needs. Perhaps worst of all, since they usually stay for a few months only, the child suffers the bewildering, if not traumatic, experience of being looked after by a succession of such girls who bring with them the differing expectations and habits of their own national cultures.

Preschool playgroups have as their most distinctive, indeed unique, feature the active involvement of mothers, not only in the planning but in the organization and day-to-day running of the groups. However they operate on a part-time basis only and, like nursery schools and classes, adopt the same long holidays as schools. For both these reasons they are of limited use to families in the greatest social need. Even where some mothers are given the opportunity to undergo some basic training and then become paid auxiliary staff, neither the hours nor the remuneration are likely to be adequate; nor is this solution possible for the majority.

Nursery schools and classes provide a rich and stimulating environment which the children are encouraged to explore, with an emphasis on self-directed activities. However, like the educational system itself, this approach is most appropriate to the middle-class child from a stimulating, concerned and interested home. Such a regime is not necessarily as appropriate to the socially deprived or otherwise handicapped.

Indeed the recent widespread advocacy of preschool education may well lead to eventual disappointment, once the promised expansion has taken place. Too much is expected from it. This is similar to the hopes which were pinned on the provision of free secondary education, on the abolition of the selection examination at the age of 11, and on comprehensive education. All were seen as giving greatly enhanced chances of equal opportunities to children from working-class homes. Now it has become evident that none has succeeded either in markedly increasing the proportion of children from such homes reaching universities or in markedly decreasing the incidence of educational backwardness. This is true not only for this country, but for many other developed countries.

Are there then any theoretical or practical justifications for quite separate and different types of preschool care and education? If the basic aim is fostering optimal, all-round development; if every existing type of provision has some advantages as well as disadvantages; if the needs of children and their families are not static but liable to change, both accidentally and intentionally; if categorizing children according to home background, economic need, ability or other criteria is socially divisive and educationally unwarranted at this early age; if easy access to services ensures

readier uptake by those most in need of them; if every child needs b
and education; then every advantage would seem to lie with setting up
comprehensive preschool centres on a neighbourhood basis.

A further advantage of such centres would be flexibility. The most
suitable programme for any one child at a particular time could be worked
out on the basis of careful initial observation and assessment. Then the
balance between physical care, mothering, stimulation, self-directed
exploration and adult-directed learning activities could be determined and
readjusted in the light of progress made; so could the frequency and length
of time the child attends.

The degree and nature of the mother's (and father's) participation in
the centre's activities could similarly be flexible but would always be
actively encouraged. In this way, preschool centres would combine the best
features of day nurseries, playgroups and nursery schools.

Research on Early Childhood

There is an urgent need for more long-term studies, both of small-scale,
intensive kinds, and of large-scale surveys. Much basic knowledge about
child development is still lacking. Moreover, we know more about
deviancy than normality; more about the conditions associated with poor
speech or reading than about how language or reading skills are normally
acquired. It is also vital to study the nature of those 'critical' events, experiences or child-rearing practices in early life which shape development.

That early stimulation or deprivation are potent and often have lasting
effects has been amply documented by work with both animals and humans.
What is lacking is an adequate methodology for promoting or reversing the
resulting consequences. It is evident by now that short-term programmes,
like Headstart or Educational Priority Area preschool schemes, have so far
shown relatively limited improvement. And even this appears to fade after
two years or so. This fact has already resulted in a powerful backlash which
argues either for genetic inferiority or for a return to more formal educational methods.

A more appropriate and rational conclusion would be to recognize
what should have been evident from the beginning: a temporary infusion of
enrichment cannot be expected to have a lasting effect on a child who
continues to live in disadvantaged circumstances. Only a continuing programme of enrichment throughout his school life has any hope of achieving
permanent results.

The longstanding neglect of developmental studies is reflected in the
fact that there is not one university department of child development in

Britain devoted solely to this vital subject (leaving aside medical departments of child health and the one chair which has a real bias towards handicap and care of deprived children).

Of course some research in universities and elsewhere is devoted to this age group as well as to child development in general; but it is short-term, atomistic, sporadic and fragmented. Funds are difficult to come by. With a few notable exceptions, the emphasis is on cognitive aspects. Multi-disciplinary investigations of young children are conspicuous by their absence.

The proposed multi-purpose preschool centres would provide ready-made laboratories for multi-disciplinary action programmes of research for the study of a wide range of issues, theoretical and practical.

So far psychologists in this country have been far too little concerned with practice-orientated research in child development, again with notable exceptions. It is perhaps indicative that the British Psychological Society established a section of developmental psychology only as recently as December 1972. Not unexpectedly psychologists as a profession have been largely divorced from policy-making.

Much remains to be learned about how to lay the foundation during the preschool years, necessary to enable children to achieve eventually the fullest measure of their potential. Yet enough is already known to take some action now. A variety of strategies will have to be explored: for promoting optimal emotional, social and intellectual development; for preventing neglect and deprivation; and, most difficult of all, for breaking into the vicious circle of the emotionally or intellectually deprived children of today becoming tomorrow's parents of yet another generation of deprived children.

Further Reading

CRELLIN, E., PRINGLE, M.K. and WEST, P. (1971) *Born Illegitimate*, NFER.

DAVIE, R., BUTLER, N. and GOLDSTEIN, H. (1972) *From Birth to Seven*, Longman and the NCB.

HALSEY, A.H. (Ed.) (1972) *Educational Priority: Vol. I, EPA Problems and Policies*, HMSO.

HUSEN, T. (1972) *Social Background and Educational Career: Research Perspectives on Equality of Educational Opportunity*, OECD.

PRINGLE, M.K. *Deprivation and Education*, (1971) (2nd edition) Longman and the NCB.

Chapter 5

Cooperation in Child and Family Care*

The Traditional Concept

The traditional meaning of the term 'child care' tends to be very circumscribed. It is mainly confined to children for whom substitute care has to be arranged because of the inability, inadequacy, or absence of parental care, be this temporary or permanent.

This traditional concept has a number of advantages: for example, services and workers can become specialized so that the needs of children can be considered specifically and separately from those of other groups, such as the elderly. Indeed, it would be most regrettable if this advantage were lost in any Seebohm reorganization. However, there are some disadvantages in this traditional concept. Two of these might be singled out because their effects influence the whole outlook, orientation and methods of the present-day child care services.

First, as it is predominantly concerned with the breakdown of the family, it is geared primarily to the socially most inadequate section of the community. So it is almost entirely a 'rescuing' service for a limited section of the child population. Thus in the public, and possibly also the professional mind it is associated with negative concepts of ineffectiveness, rejection and failure.

Secondly, the child care service still tends to be called upon at times of crisis when intervention is a matter of urgency. A service geared to crises inevitably assumes the features appropriate to emergency situations: flexibility, resourcefulness, improvization and a sense of urgency are the positive features; but on the negative side, long-term planning, careful matching of child to provision, re-education and evaluation inevitably play a minor part.

*This paper, an expanded version of a talk at the Annual Conference of the Association of Children's Officers, 1969, was originally published in the Bureau's journal *Concern*, 5, 1970, pp. 4–16.

The Literal Concept

Would there be advantages in adopting the literal meaning of child care? Used in this sense, it encompasses something at once much broader and more positive. All children need to be cared for; and, at one time or another of their lives, almost every child needs very special care.

Such a view of child care cuts across all the barriers which surround the traditional concept; barriers of social class, of professional training and discipline, of local government organization, of central government departments and the like. A preventive outlook is not just added on, but built in, as is the idea of adopting a long-term perspective, rather than acting on an ad hoc basis according to pressing circumstances in the here-and-now.

The time seems ripe for changing the concept of child care in this way. Why? Because the professions themselves are changing their basic aims. Over-simplifying, it could be said that initially medicine aimed at curing the sick; education at eradicating ignorance; and social work at rescuing the social failure. Thus all three professions were largely orientated towards 'disease' or deficiencies.

Now a change is taking place and its direction is parallel in the three professional fields: particular symptoms (in medicine), needs (in social work) or skills and subjects (in education) are no longer seen as the main targets of professional attention; instead, positive good health, the education of the 'whole child', and the strengthening of the individual in relation to society, have become the main professional aims. Not only are aims becoming similar, but each profession is beginning to draw on concepts and insights developed by the others, as well as by related disciplines, such as psychology, psychiatry, sociology and anthropology.

As far as 'vulnerable' children and their families are concerned, concepts and aims are almost identical: to prevent, or at least ameliorate, the consequences of potentially harmful conditions. The broad categories of children 'at risk' are now generally agreed upon; there are six groups, and these are, of course, not mutually exclusive:

1 Large families with low incomes;
2 families where personal relationships are impaired;
3 one-parent families;
4 those affected by serious or irreversible physical or mental illness, or a disabling handicap;
5 families affected by sudden crises;
6 children who have to live apart from their families for longer or shorter periods.

'Vulnerable' children and their families are usually known to doctors, teachers and social workers in an area because they make greater, more frequent, and more complex demands on all available services. Thus cooperation could well begin in relation to this group which may comprise as high a proportion as 20 per cent of all families.

Of course, each profession will retain and develop further its own skills, expertise and body of theoretical knowledge. But a common goal may strengthen the desire for cooperation as well as provide the impetus towards achieving it. What then is the common goal in child care, using the term in the literal sense? To enable each child to develop his full potential for physical, intellectual, emotional and social growth; and in the case of the 'vulnerable' child, to minimize the ill-effects of any adverse conditions.

Is Cooperation Working Effectively?

Views may differ depending on individual experience. But overall perhaps we can agree that so far it has not been a conspicuous success. There are several possible reasons why this is so. Two are worth mentioning. First, that it may be too early to judge, partly because no systematic evidence is as yet available. Secondly, that cooperation has hitherto been attempted on too limited an assumption; namely, that health, education and child care services have different aims, though there are certain areas of common concern; hence, it is said, coordination is needed.

Instead, a much wider basis is suggested: namely, that the major services for children have similar aims and hence an integrated approach is needed rather than merely coordination. Is this a feasible proposition?

There are several examples of an integrated approach outside the local authority structure. Large business firms, such as Marks and Spencer or ICI, universities and even government services such as the GPO or the armed forces, accept implicitly that the health, education and training, as well as the personal and social well-being of their employees, students or members, are their responsibility. Hence they each provide their own integrated organization of services.

Is this parallel justified or is local government essentially different? It could be argued that the examples given deal with small units; their members are more homogenous or in some way selected; they are primarily concerned with adults; and they serve a definite function or a narrower purpose. None of these, except perhaps the last, stand up to closer examination. In any case, no analogy can be pressed too far.

How to Move Towards Cooperation in Child Care

To call for an integrated approach as a real basis for cooperation, is not to advocate a complete merging of the different services into one monolithic kind of 'super-service'. Nor do I think that the day-to-day functions of health, education and child care work need to be integrated. It is the overall policies and priorities which need to be worked out.

Can any changes be set in train now towards some measure of integrated endeavour? Two areas seem particularly suitable to try out these suggestions: diagnosis and assessment on the one hand, and preventive work on the other.

Comprehensive Diagnostic Facilities

It is comparatively rare now to find a child with a single handicapping condition. This is due partly to greater diagnostic skill and awareness; also to a greater recognition of the importance of emotional factors; and partly to advances in medical knowledge, which are having the twin effects of eliminating or reducing the incidence of certain defects, while enabling a greater number of severely damaged children to survive. So we now recognize that handicaps overlap: the incidence of educationally backward children is high among the socially and culturally deprived; physically handicapped children often have emotional difficulties; among maladjusted children learning difficulties are very common; and there is a high incidence of educational failure among juvenile delinquents.

Yet diagnosis of these different groups is undertaken in different establishments: in remand homes or classifying schools (or sometimes both) for delinquents; in assessment centres or diagnostic units for those who are physically handicapped; in child guidance clinics or school psychological services for emotionally disturbed or educationally backward children; and in reception centres for children who are received into care.

Yet the basic team needed for diagnostic work of any kind is the same: a doctor, a psychologist and a social worker. This basic team may need to be supplemented in particular cases by speech therapists, neurologists, or remedial teachers, to mention just a few. Because there is a shortage of every type of trained staff, even existing diagnostic facilities are not always working at full strength, nor do all children who need it receive an adequate initial diagnostic examination.

Would, therefore, some pooling and integration of available diagnostic resources mark a step forward? In addition to their more effective use, a more comprehensive, and at the same time more efficient, pattern of diagnosis and prognosis might be evolved. Also, smaller authorities, who cannot establish every type of diagnostic facility, would be enabled to set up at least one comprehensive diagnostic unit.

If the cost were borne jointly by the local authority committees, primarily responsible for children, the burden on any one would be less onerous. But because this work requires highly trained and experienced staff, it can never be cheap. Yet inappropriate treatment, caused by a lack of proper diagnostic facilities, is likely to be even more expensive in the long run.

Preventive Work

Here, very different levels of knowledge prevail in medicine, child care and education. The advances which can be achieved have been impressively demonstrated by a wide range of environmental health services which have brought about a revolution in children's physical health and development within the short span of thirty years.

In child care a preventive approach is of comparatively recent origin. Though the Children and Young Persons Act, 1963, has given it impetus education has only recently accepted the need for remedial work. And it is more recently still that the need for compensatory education has been recognized. Prevention, however, still does not play much part in educational thinking.

Now there is new knowledge which can provide a common starting point for the medical, child care and education services: we know that the most basic and most important learning — in the intellectual, emotional and social field alike — takes place during the first few years of a child's life. Thus there is a common aim: to prevent intellectual, emotional and educational neglect; or to put it positively, to promote emotional resilience and to develop learning potential. This common aim could provide the basis for a comprehensive, integrated, preventive approach.

The current vogue is to stress 'cost effectiveness'. This gives the impression of scientific rigour but in fact ignores the central issue of fundamental goals and values. It is these which should determine how to choose from possible alternative courses of action. Cost effectiveness as the main criterion is a poor instrument for determining priorities: it is short-sighted and restrictive. Furthermore, the long-established political and bureaucratic habit of fragmented, departmentalized decision-making inevitably leads to a preference for setting up child care provision rather than determining first how best to care for children in our modern society — all children, and not only those who are vulnerable or have special needs.

Children's basic needs have not, of course, changed. Affection, security, new experiences and recognition for achievement are the essential prerequisites for emotional and intellectual development, in short for learning. In recent years, the demands on human capacity to learn and to make new adjustments have increased, both in scope and speed. When it took a generation or more for social and other changes to come about, the human personality could adapt itself gradually and slowly.

Contemporary changes are much more rapid and radical. The pace of technological and scientific progress is such that professional knowledge and skills become out of date in a matter of years. Social and moral values are also in the melting pot, now that traditional religious beliefs are losing their influence and society is becoming more egalitarian, socially mobile and non-authoritarian.

Because change implies a threat to security, it tends to produce anxiety and aggressive resentment. Yet to face and cope adequately with change demands increased security and the ability to tolerate uncertainty. If the gap between the generations is greater than before, may this be because the scope and speed of change has left adults more uncertain of their own values?

Be this as it may, it looks as if the most essential personal qualities children will need to acquire are adaptability, flexibility and resilience. These will enable them to make rapid and radical new adjustments and to tolerate more effectively the stresses which this inevitably entails. How can we help children to achieve this? By providing for them an environment, rich in experience and experiment; rich in security and affection; while at the same time, there need to be opportunities for decision, for choice and for the resolution of conflict. Parents, teachers and all others who come into contact with the young, can no longer hope to provide them with a map of the future; only with honest interpretations of the present and some sign-posts to a future, which they themselves cannot envisage with any degree of certainty.

It seems imperative to accept, as a starting point, that forms of social and psychological adjustment, which have hitherto proved satisfactory, will not suffice for the future. Immediate changes in our educational and child caring practices are essential. In what follows, I shall suggest how this could be done for each age group; the preschool, the school age and the adolescent child and his family.

The Preschool Years

This period is of fundamental importance to all later development. The child has to learn more during the first few years of life than during any other comparable timespan; also this learning provides the basis for all later progress. Hence proportionately much greater attention — in terms of time, money and other resources — must be given to this early period. How well he will get on with authority figures and contemporaries; whether he will come to regard new problems as a challenge or a threat; how successful he will be scholastically; these are just a few examples of the many tasks of childhood, the mastery or failure of which depends to a very considerable extent on the opportunities the child has had available in these most formative, early years.

In themselves these opportunities are simple: mutually satisfying, dependable and affectionate relationships within a stable family setting; rich opportunities for play; and a wide range of experiences which promote intellectual and language development. Through being loved and valued unconditionally, for his own sake, he learns to live with himself and with others. Through environmental stimulation, he learns how to learn.

The remarkable improvement in children's physical health and growth witnessed during the past thirty years has come about chiefly in two ways: first by a wide dissemination of knowledge, such as the importance of early diet, regular checks on weight, and so on; secondly, by making generally available to all mothers, irrespective of class or income, easy access to guidance and advice on physical health through infant welfare centres.

The analogy is obvious: there is little doubt that in all strata of society the level of children's emotional stability and intellectual growth could be significantly raised; if for no other reason, because we know now so much more about some of the means by which these can be fostered than we did even twenty years ago. To do so will require a similar campaign, cooperatively planned and executed by educators, psychologists, social workers, doctors and health visitors — indeed, all who come into contact with the preschool child and his family. The mass media, too, particularly television, the most powerful of them all, could play a vital role.

Below the age of two or three years infant welfare centres would be most suited to serve as the focus for this educational task; but their orientation would need to change towards making available guidance and advice on the emotional and intellectual needs of children. After the early months of a baby's life, the health visitor becomes a very infrequent caller if things are going well. It must come to be accepted instead that the earliest years of infancy give mothers (and fathers) a unique and essential opportunity to provide the most important and the most basic education their children will ever receive. On it all later success depends. Paediatricians, paediatric nurses and health visitors could undertake the task of spreading this knowledge and ensuring that it is translated into practice. However, their own training would need to be refocused to equip them for this task.

Between the ages of two to five years nursery school could become the focus for the services concerned with the care of children. Then teachers would largely be responsible for parent guidance and for actively involving mothers in their children's learning. Other professional workers, doctors, nurses and child care officers, could also use the nursery school as their base.

However, by itself greater parental understanding of the various stages of normal child development and of how it can best be fostered, is not sufficient. Social planners, architects, housing and child welfare authorities must ensure the provision of the means for meeting the needs of young children, particularly in urban areas. This can only be achieved by their close cooperation with the consumers, parents and teachers alike.

The 'Vulnerable' Preschool Child

Here the keynote must be early and constructive intervention. If the integrated service for preschool children was available, it would have another important task, namely to operate what might be called an early warning system. Children 'at risk' would not only be known, but their progress and family situation would be under constant and regular review. Special help could be made available early; it would be constructive in the sense that the intervention would aim at enabling the child or family to cope independently at the earliest opportunity. At the same time it must be accepted, that some vulnerable families may need long-term support if they are to be contained within the community as a reasonably well-functioning unit.

At times of crisis young children are particularly vulnerable. A great expansion of ancillary services, such as adequate home help during the mother's confinement or illness, would immediately lessen the need to separate little children from their families. Every year many thousands have to be taken into care for these reasons alone. A corps of home helpers could also be of considerable benefit to mothers of seriously handicapped children. Given some regular relief from the burden of unremitting care, many might be enabled to cope and, indeed, wish to do so rather than opt for institutional care. To do so it must be shown that being a home help is not simply a superior type of domestic but it means giving a vital social service. This in turn implies better status and pay.

The child from a socially and culturally underprivileged home is adversely affected from an early age and cumulatively thereafter. His parents are usually ill-educated, if not of limited ability, so all too often he becomes intellectually neglected or deprived. If equal educational opportunity for all children is to be more than an attractive slogan, positive discrimination is essential. How to do so, indeed how effectively this can be done is still an open question. What is beyond doubt is that opportunities for language development must be provided during the early preschool years. Such opportunities surround the child in the educated, literate home; without them the culturally deprived child has lost the educational race long before starting school. On the lowest level of national self-interest, this results in a loss of intellectual potential which society cannot afford.

Another particularly vulnerable group are children who suffer from some physical or mental defect. To prevent it from becoming a handicap, early detection, parent guidance and their active cooperation in treatment are essential. Appropriate opportunities for early learning are also crucial. Nursery schools should be closely involved in what must be a continuous process of early diagnosis, prognosis, teaching and reassessment. These could be special ones such as the Catherine Elliott School in Shropshire, or those who as a matter of policy accept a proportion of handicapped children, as well as home teachers with special training. Such provision, if evaluated, will further our as yet limited knowledge of the most effective methods of early compensatory education for the various types of handicap.

The Middle Years of Childhood

The only professional service which is in contact with all children for at least a ten-year span is the school. Thus it could well serve as the focal point from which caring for children radiates during this period.

Education, it used to be thought, was primarily a matter of imparting basic skills of a mainly intellectual kind as well as furthering children's personal development. New psychological insights — about individual differences, about the nature of intelligence, about the sequential stages in reasoning, about group dynamics and about learning theory — have had profound effects both on the curriculum and on teaching methods, especially at the primary stage of education. The ability and desire to find out and to apply knowledge to new situations, is being seen as a vital part of the educational process. Hence teachers have become less subject orientated and more child-centred; this in turn has also led to greater concern with the environment from which pupils are drawn.

Now schools are extending their role to include more personal contact with parents; more educational guidance as well as remedial work with children who have special needs; and closer contact with the social, especially the child care, services. Teachers could well become the 'general practitioners' in child and family life. Their knowledge of normal growth and development should enable them on the one hand to counsel parents, both formally and informally; and on the other hand, to operate an early warning system by calling in as consultants the various psychological, medical or child care workers. If things went wrong, then one or other of these special services might have to take over responsibility. In the great majority of cases, however, their specialist skills and expertise would be used in an advisory capacity only, to improve the knowledge and thus increase the general level of child care.

The 'Vulnerable Child', Aged 5–12

How best to supplement inadequate parental care and compensate for environmental deprivation while the child remains with his own family, needs experiment and study. A variety of educational and community programmes are being tried in the United States and in Israel, as well as in this country. Special remedial provision; day classes and schools for children with adjustment difficulties; supervised adventure playgrounds; clubs linked with, as well as separate from, schools; holiday camps and the French idea of colonies de vacances; experiments like Northorpe Hall; these are just some of the ways which widen a child's horizon and keep him constructively occupied during weekends and holidays.

It should be recognized that the child who must be removed from his own home, needs the most highly skilled substitute care if he is to be rehabilitated. All residential facilities, whether hostels, homes, special schools or approved schools, must become remedial and therapeutic communities. The basic fact is simple: loving care is not enough, while a mainly custodial regime evades the real issues.

The time has come to recognize, as is done in education, that some children are in need of 'special care', temporarily or permanently. To do so might lead to making removal from home a more rational and positive procedure, as well as to avoid the rather meaningless labels which are used at present for children who are emotionally and socially deprived or damaged.

The Adolescent

The period from 12 to 17 years might be regarded as a second weaning from dependence on parents and authority figures. Puberty and physical maturity are reached earlier now; yet full-time and part-time education have been steadily extended, thus prolonging the period of dependence on parents. But the main growth tasks facing adolescents have remained basically the same. They cover four main areas: occupational choice; social behaviour especially in relation to becoming emancipated from dependence on parental authority; sexual adjustment; and finding some interpretation of life, however vague or simply formulated, which gives meaning and direction to one's behaviour and that of others.

Once again, there is a variety of unintegrated services for adolescents. For example, educational counselling and vocational guidance are not only separate but rarely adequate in scope and often start too late. A large number of young people are quite unprepared for the abrupt transition from the school environment, which is designed for their benefit, to the factory, shop or office where they are regarded as a replaceable cipher of economic rather than personal value.

For the child whose earlier years have been deprived — emotionally, socially or intellectually — adolescence will bring both greater dangers and greater opportunities. Greater dangers because his early experiences are likely to have left him immature, insecure and less resilient; greater opportunities because adolescence offers a second chance, as it were, to make satisfying, mutually rewarding relationships with significant adults outside the immediate family.

Any adult closely concerned with the care of adolescents — be he a teacher, youth leader, child care worker, probation officer or employer — can have a profound influence on their personality development. To do so, he must be willing to make a warm and caring relationship in which the child is enabled to learn more adequately what was denied him in earlier years. The unloved, rejected adolescent has failed to learn to make satisfying relationships. He has grown as impervious to affection and kindness, as to disapproval and punishment; to that extent he is 'unreachable'. Strict discipline and severe punishment may temporarily succeed in outwardly containing a social or antisocial behaviour; but as soon as these controls are relaxed or can be evaded, it becomes evident that no change has taken place.

Fortunately the number of affectionless, unreachable adolescents is small, but they present a major challenge: partly because the problem of how and whether they can be helped has not yet been solved; and partly because the facilities for attempting this task are woefully inadequate.

The Way Ahead for Cooperation in Child and Family Care

A greatly expanded research programme is needed and, since the child is father to the man, this might seem a sensible starting point. The fact that central government devotes over 50 per cent of its research budget to aviation alone and a fraction of 1 per cent to child development, is merely one indication of currently accepted, national priorities.

Just as a breakthrough in knowledge occurred when various physical and biological sciences joined in studying the same problems, so all the social sciences must learn to work together to solve the complex problems of human motivation. For example, there are a number of theories derived from psychology, sociology, education and psychiatry, regarding conditions likely to lead to persistent juvenile delinquency. But none has attempted to answer the practically much more important question why a youngster does not become delinquent despite being similarly handicapped by personal and environmental conditions. Such questions will only be solved by multi-disciplinary and long-term enquiries concerned with unselected large groups of children.

Some will argue that experiments where children and their families are concerned, are unethical. But if all the appropriate safeguards are provided (such as the preservation of anonymity and the avoidance of measures known to have harmful effects) surely the opposite is the case? It is unethical not to do so. If the welfare society has a duty to help the deprived it also has an obligation to provide the most effective help. What is needed is:

1. to evaluate past research; replicate small scale enquiries in different places; and co-ordinate existing research;
2. to mount a series of long-term enquiries;
3. and to set in train operational and development work so that experimental schemes and ideas can be properly worked through and evaluated.

Much evaluation and research could be carried out by child care, education and medical services themselves, given expert guidance.

For full effectiveness on a regional or national basis, however, methods of record keeping would need to be improved and rationalized. Busy practitioners will continue to be impatient with 'all that paperwork' so long as 'much that is already collected is stored undisturbed by human thought' (Peterson *et al, Lancet,* 1967, p. 771). Once it is seen that records are used to gain further knowledge and to improve practice, time would more readily be given to them.

All those professionally concerned with children deplore the lack of trained staff and the general shortage of personnel. Yet there is little hope of a sudden or dramatic improvement. Other possibilities thus deserve serious consideration. Let me mention three. First, greater coordination among existing services is likely to lead to a more effective deployment of available resources.

Secondly, there is a relatively untapped reservoir of labour for professional or semi-professional employment: namely, married women who have children old enough to make part-time study and work possible. A wider range of more imaginatively conceived training courses could be provided to take into account the fact that mothers possess several years' practical experience of child rearing and family management. It is both wasteful and stultifying to model training courses on those available for pupils straight from school. Also employers will need to offer married women flexible hours so that domestic responsibilities could more readily be dovetailed with work outside the home.

Thirdly, greatly increased community involvement in caring for children could contribute to easing present-day staff shortages. There are signs that students and older school children increasingly consider such involvement as a worthwhile challenge; recent years have also seen the emergence of influential organizations founded by parents of children with special needs. Thus, a more broadly based ideal of community service in tune with a more egalitarian, socially mobile society, is beginning to emerge.

Of course, there are difficulties in each of these three possibilities, but they are less intractable than coping with chronic and severe staff shortages. Otherwise how can the vicious circle be broken of too few staff, unable to give their best because of inadequate conditions, which in turn makes many leave, thus leading to a worse staffing situation?

Community Work

Since this has now become a very fashionable concept, it carries with it the danger of over-commitment in the sense that too much is claimed and expected from it; as a result there could well be a backlash. As I see it the essential difference, indeed contrast to traditional practice, lies in two factors: first, there is participation by those for whom the service is intended; and secondly prevention rather than rescue or rehabilitation, is the primary aim. Taken together these imply much greater cooperation at every level and between all the disciplines.

The traditional training in medicine, education and social work makes the practitioner aware that he must exercise his authority and instruct his patient/pupils/clients in what to do; thus people have things done to or for them, rather than being helped by the practitioner to become able to do things by and for themselves. Hence throughout his training period an authoritarian attitude is built into the practitioner which is then reinforced by the hierarchical structure of all the services concerned. It is not surprising then that considerable resistance is being met by those who are attempting to change the present pattern of practice. Thus it is considered a daring experiment when one teaching hospital is setting up a unit in which patients with serious kidney diseases actively participate in their own management and treatment by reporting on symptoms, on the effects of drugs and so on; schools which have introduced project methods, have given up streaming and are child centred, are being subjected to largely unsubstantiated attack; and social workers who identify themselves closely with the legitimate grievances of their clients, say with regard to housing needs, find themselves in a serious conflict of loyalty vis-à-vis their employers. Participation is inevitably beset by problems which need to be openly acknowledged, faced and worked through, by all concerned including elected members and other employing authorities.

Changing over from an authoritarian to a participating framework is also bewildering to the recipient, be he pupil, client or patient, and thus initially there may well be uncertainty, confusion and sometimes chaos. The danger is that these difficulties may lead to a premature decision to give up a new approach.

On the positive side there is mounting evidence that even those families considered culturally deprived, financially impoverished and otherwise handicapped, have greater resources of self-help and insight than have hitherto been suspected. This has been demonstrated in, for example, the Bureau's study of Family Advice Services in high-need areas.

Pitfalls in Participation and Self-Help

Situations will inevitably arise where an individual or community decide to discriminate against a particular group, such as coloured immigrants, or to be self-destructive, by the use of drugs, alcohol, etc. How can prejudiced or self-destructive attitudes be combatted? There are no easy answers. On the one hand the worker must make it clear that he disapproves of the decision or action of the group or individual, but on the other hand, he must avoid doing what society has always done and continues to do, namely to reject not only the deed but also the doer. This means making clear the thin, yet very real, dividing line between disapproval of certain attitudes or actions while continuing to accept the individual or the community concerned.

Nor does acceptance mean excusing or condoning. Rather it implies the recognition that if changes are to be brought about, they will come in the main through the pupil's, client's or patient's trust and ability to see the relevance, and often advantages, of different ways of behaviour. Of course, outward conformity can be more or less readily enforced. But no-one, not even the youngest child, can ever be made to conform when 'authority' is not watching unless he does so of his own free will. Yet this obvious truth is still too often ignored by all members of the helping professions, let alone the lay person, be he parent or volunteer helper.

Pitfalls in Using Volunteers

An increasing involvement with the community on equal terms seems to have been accompanied, or possibly even been stimulated by, a more broadly based concept of voluntary service. If such a concept were to become a living reality among lower middle-class and working-class people, it could narrow the 'social gap' between those who are giving and those who are at the receiving end; also barriers of communication and distrust might be lowered in this way.

If a great increase in voluntary helpers is to be absorbed smoothly into the fabric of the social, educational and medical services, a number of difficulties will have to be overcome. One of these lies in the resistance of professional workers which ranges from condescension and suspicion, to hostility and outright rejection. On the other hand, the volunteer may tend to feel superior to the professional: he can be seen as being less altruistic and emotionally committed because he does a paid job. Both attitudes will need to be modified to obviate unproductive friction.

Another difficult issue is how to make the best use of the untrained volunteer in a world of increasingly complex professionalism. What jobs is he to do? If only the simplest, dullest or most menial tasks are allocated to him, his enthusiasm is unlikely to last long. Yet the most challenging tasks usually require a high degree of skill. Is the volunteer to be given some systematic induction as well as continued instruction and inservice training? That there must be some continuous supervision and consultation with the professional worker is generally agreed but thought is needed on how often, by whom and in what ways this is best done.

New patterns of cooperation are likely to develop when it has become generally accepted that the consolidation and expansion of all services for the family in general and children in particular depend on the contribution of both professional and voluntary workers. Even if training were greatly expanded it is unlikely that there will ever be enough doctors, teachers and social workers to give all the help and services required. This must not become an excuse for using volunteers simply as a source of cheap labour or as a stopgap in a time of financial stringency. What needs to be done is to delineate how each can most usefully complement and supplement the contribution of the other to the greatest advantage of those they are serving.

Needless to say this is a complex task for which there are no absolutely right solutions but only a range of approximations appropriate for different places and settings.

The Way Ahead

Much remains to be learned about how best to promote children's development; but enough is known already to take action. If even half of what is now known were accepted with feeling and carried out with understanding by all who have the care of children, the revolution brought about in children's physical health might well be matched. There can be little doubt that improved psychological care would result in strengthening children's emotional resilience and increasing their capacity for learning. The development of an integrated system of communication and cooperation between all professionally concerned with children, would make services more effectively available to parents. A network of early warning systems would make prevention a practical possibility. Its orientation must be broad: to strengthen and promote family functioning within a supportive community.

Chapter 6

Deprivation and Education*

Introduction

Deprivation has many faces: the child who grows up in a home which is culturally and educationally unstimulating is handicapped by environmental deprivation; the child who is unloved and rejected by his parents suffers emotional deprivation; and the child who lives in residential care, for long periods or permanently, is deprived of normal family life. These three conditions are not, of course, mutually exclusive, and there are also other kinds of deprivation which affect education. But I shall confine myself to these three situations, not least because they are of most immediate relevance to those working in the residential child care field.

Education is usually thought of in terms of what schools are aiming to provide. Yet how successful a child is within this more formal setting depends almost entirely on how successful his informal learning has been in the preceding years. Learning in the widest and yet most basic sense of the word begins at birth — every change, from the utter helplessness of the new-born baby to the comparative competence of the toddler and young infant, is due to learning. Maturation plays an essential part but it is of little avail without environmental opportunity. For example, if a baby remains confined in a cot he will not learn to walk, and unless he hears human speech he will not learn to talk, even though he is in all other ways ready to do so.

Neither opportunity for learning nor maturational readiness are, however, sufficient by themselves. To these two ingredients a third must be added: motivation or a willingness to learn. This desire to learn is the essential driving force which has its spring in the quality of relationships available to the child. Fortunate is the child who is loved unconditionally by

*From *Education, The Annual Review of the Residential Child Care Association*, 1971–72, 19, 1972, pp. 16–24. (The RCCA is now called Social Care Association.)

his parents, who set before him standards of behaviour and achievement which are reasonable in the light of his age and ability; and who provide an environment which is culturally and educationally stimulating.

Children who come into residential care have rarely been so fortunate. Recent evidence shows that even those who experience short-term care have got off to a poor start from the very beginning of their life; and throughout at least their first seven years, they continue to be a disadvantaged group (Mapstone, 1969). As one would predict, this then affects their educational progress and adjustment at school. This close link between deprivation and education was similarly shown in a series of studies relating to seven-, eleven- and fifteen-year olds (Pringle, 1971).

Why should this be so? And what can houseparents do to reverse or at least mitigate the effects of past deprivation? In trying to answer these questions, I will first show how and why willingness to learn is so closely interwoven with the quality of emotional relationships; i.e. the link between learning and emotion. Then I will describe our new understanding of the nature of intelligence which has a central bearing on remedial action. And finally I will suggest ways in which residential care can become a positive, constructive and therapeutic experience.

Emotion and Learning

How children learn was for a long time considered mainly in the narrow context of scholastic achievement. Now we know that it all starts very early. So early that, like the proverbial chicken and egg question, it is academic to ask which comes first, learning or emotion. A baby begins to learn from the day he is born and from this day, too, he is affected by parental, particularly maternal love. At best such love is unconditional: he is valued for his own sake and not because he is a boy or girl, fair or dark, attractive or plain. This caring affection is so all-pervasive that it communicates itself to him in everything his mother does for him.

Through being loved, the baby learns to feel love for her and goes on to learn what is involved in making a relationship with another person; that it implies not only receiving but also giving affection; not only making demands but willingness to satisfy the demands of others; no longer expecting immediate satisfaction but being willing to accept the frustration of delay; and being prepared to subordinate one's wishes to those of others instead of being completely self-centred.

Because of this reciprocal bond he perseveres with learning to be dry and clean, to walk, to talk and eventually to succeed with school learning. If this early experience of love has been lacking, if he has been rejected or deprived, his learning will remain slow, difficult and often inadequate. According to his temperament, he will either be apathetic or unresponsive, or he will fight and protest against every new demand made upon him.

The unconditionally accepted and loved child learns three basic lessons: a pleasurable awareness of his own identity, his self; the joy of a mutually rewarding relationship; and a desire for approval, which acts as a spur to learning.

Thus the pleasure of his parents in his progress provides the main incentive for his learning. Later, the approval of other adults important to him is the chief motivating force which makes him want to conform to expectations, to acquire new skills, respond to more taxing tasks and to master more complex knowledge — in short, to learn. The most important of these other adults are parent substitutes and then teachers.

It is because relationships with significant adults, and later with the peer group, provide both the incentive and the conditions for learning, that emotional disturbance and educational failure often follow similar paths. The rejected child is deprived not only of affection but simultaneously of the most effective incentive for learning. Hence he frequently becomes both backward and maladjusted.

The Nature of Intelligence

It used to be thought of as something rather like height — determined from the start, as it were, and unchanging once it was fully developed; hence some children were bright, the majority middling or average, and others were destined to be slow learners. Now we know that it is much more complex. Whatever a child's intellectual potential, it will only be realized if the right kind of stimulation — 'mental food' if you like — is provided. Thus the environment can make or mar, retard or promote, the development of intelligence, that is the ability to learn.

This ability needs to be nourished, from the word 'go', just as the body does. And in the same way, what happens during the earliest years of childhood is the most crucial: in the physical field about half of the eventual adult stature is attained between conception and the age of two and a half years; while from conception to the age of four years, half of the total intellectual growth takes place.

What then is the necessary 'mental food' to which I referred? Its very ordinariness leads us to underestimate its vital importance. It consists of exploration, play and language. All normal children have a strong urge to explore, to welcome the challenge of new situations and to gain a sense of achievement from eventual mastery. This urge to find out persists — or at least, can and should persist — throughout life. Yet for the majority of children who are received into care it does not do so. Why?

Evidence has been accumulating on the damaging effects of a culturally impoverished or deprived environment on intellectual growth. This is a home — be it with a small or capital H — which fails to provide the necessary 'intellectual food' to develop the child's potential to the fullest extent (Dinnage and Pringle, 1967; Crellin, Pringle and West, 1971; Pringle, 1971). Without the necessary diet of rich opportunities for play and for language development, the ability to learn remains stunted. The consequences are most severe and all-pervasive during the earliest years of childhood. It is then that the basis is laid for speech development, for problem solving, for independent thinking, in short, for learning how to learn; and perhaps most important of all, it is again during the preschool years that parental expectation and stimulation provide the child with the motivation to want to learn.

The exact difference which an enriching or depriving home background respectively can make, needs a great deal more research. 'However, a conservative estimate of the effect of extreme environments on intelligence is about 20 IQ points. This could mean the difference between a life in an institution for the subnormal or a productive life in society. It could mean the difference between a professional career and an occupation which is at the semi-skilled or unskilled level' (Bloom, 1964).

The earliest years, then, are most basic for laying the foundation for intellectual development. Unlike physical development, however, it continues to grow until the age of about fifty years though it becomes much slower after seventeen years or thereabouts. This means that it is never 'too late'. Hence those who undertake the care of deprived children and young people need never give up hope — indeed, an optimistic attitude, a real belief in the possibility of change and improvement play an essential part in all rehabilitation. Which brings me to how residential care staff can counteract, or at least mitigate, the effects of deprivation.

Practical Implications

Just as the undernourished child requires a carefully balanced diet to build up or restore him physically, so judiciously balanced care is needed to build up or restore a deprived child's emotional health and to develop his intellectual potential. The role of the residential staff is crucial in this. How much can be achieved in reversing the effects of early deprivation has only been fully realized in recent years.

There is evidence from a variety of sources: studies of identical twins, reared apart, where the one brought up in a more favourable environment shows more favourable development than his less fortunate twin; illegitimately born children, who show much better emotional adjustment and educational attainment, when growing up in adopted homes, than those who have remained with their own mothers in a stressful, deprived environment; or immigrant children who show much higher educational achievements than their parents because they were afforded much greater opportunities in their adopted country.

In short, although the effects of an unstimulating home background, of unhappy relations between child and parents, or both, are likely to lead to emotional difficulties, stunted intellectual development and poor educational achievements, change can be brought about. As always, the earlier this is attempted the less difficult it is; and prevention is better than cure. How, then, can it be achieved?

I will discuss this separately for the different age groups, but the basic principles are, of course, the same for all children: to establish a loving, secure, mutually satisfying relationship with a caring adult; to kindle or rekindle curiosity, the desire to learn; and to provide an environment which stimulates language development and intellectual growth.

The pre-school child

The younger the child, the greater the shock of being removed from home; his inevitably limited understanding of verbal explanations adds to his bewilderment. Also a young child often feels it is his naughtiness which has led to his being sent away from home and hence being unwanted. Limited language ability remains a difficulty in the first task of restoring a sense of security, of being welcomed and valued. Establishing a personal bond of affection is the only means of doing so, but to achieve this a small staff is required where changes of personnel are kept to a minimum, especially during the initial stages. Once a secure relationship has been created with one adult, the child can then reach out to new ones.

High priority needs to be given from the outset to stimulating speech and intellectual development. The opportunities which surround a child in the educated, literate home must be provided in abundance just because they have been missing in his early days. Nursery rhymes, fairy tales, songs, and being talked to, long before he can speak himself, are essential activities; they must not be regarded as merely incidental and subsidiary to physical care, habit training and general homemaking tasks. Similarly, being played with is as essential as having suitable toys available.

Because these activities are enjoyable, not only for the child but also for the adult, they must not be regarded as a luxury and 'a bit of a waste of time'. Rather, regular daily periods should be devoted to these activities; in addition, every opportunity needs to be used during the day for conversation and verbal stimulation. Mixed age groups of children also help. In such family groups, younger children learn from and imitate older ones. Being only with one's own age group is less stimulating to language development while staff, in turn, are not faced with a whole group of toddlers all at the 'eternal questioning' stage.

Even the youngest infant should be given some personal toys. Only if exclusive ownership is granted will a toddler gradually learn to develop a sense of responsibility for his own belongings and a pride in them. Also, possessions are a talking point, as much for children as for adults. Some people contemptuously dismiss 'baby talk'. But only if we talk to babies will they outgrow the need for baby talk. The more we speak, sing and read to children, the more readily do they learn to enjoy the give-and-take of conversation with contemporaries and adults. This enjoyment and skill forms the basis for the later mastery of the three R's in school; and, more important still, for participating to an increasing extent in our predominantly verbal culture.

The middle years of childhood
How best to compensate for the effects of inadequate parental care and of environmental deprivation still needs exploration. Such rehabilitation requires the most highly skilled care if it is to succeed. The basic fact is beyond dispute: loving care is not enough, while a mainly institutional or custodial regime evades the real issues. All residential facilities, whether hostels, homes or special schools, must become remedial and therapeutic communities. Only then can removal from home become a positive, constructive means of intervention.

What the infant needs remains also a basic requirement for the older child: rewarding relationships with adults and peers, and a stimulating environment to foster his learning abilities. Stimulating here often means allowing the child to behave, to talk and to play at a level much below that of his actual age. Owing to previously experienced deprivations he is likely to be immature for his years; he needs to cover the ground which bridges the gap between where he is and where he has to get to, in order to hold his own with his contemporaries. This includes talking with and reading to him regularly, especially if he has remained poor at it himself.

In addition, specific provisions must be sought for overcoming educational and social disabilities. Like any good parent, residential staff need to find a school where remedial groups and special classes for learning difficulties are provided. Unfortunately, in too many schools these are still inadequate or non-existent. In case of unmet need, the Social Services Department can provide these facilities themselves and employ remedial teachers to give help within the residential setting. Making available remedial treatment within the residential setting of a children's Home (soon to become community homes), both for short and long-term cases, has been found to be effective over a period of years now in a number of areas (Pringle, 1971).

To coach or not to coach is a question facing many a houseparent. There is no straightforward answer. Some children prefer to forget their educational difficulties, even hide them from those whose good opinion they value; others find support in sharing their anxieties about school work with someone they trust and whose help they welcome. If help is given, it is advisable to do so in consultation with the teacher to avoid confusing the child by a different approach. In most cases it is not mere coaching which is required. Rather a compensatory programme of enriching experience which widens the child's whole horizon is needed to overcome the cumulative effects of prolonged deprivation. Often, too, this needs to be linked with a comprehensive remedial scheme.

In some cases learning difficulties may be so severe or resistant that a full psychological examination is indicated. Then the houseparent, like any good parent, should seek specialist advice. Its availability varies greatly from one part of the country to another but, given persistence and patience, it can be obtained. Though neither quick nor easy remedies can be expected, a comprehensive assessment of the child's strengths and weaknesses, and an appropriate treatment programme are of great help.

The adolescent

For the child whose earlier years have been deprived — emotionally or intellectually — adolescence brings greater dangers and greater opportunities. Greater dangers because his early experiences are likely to have left him immature, insecure and educationally adrift; greater opportunities because he has now a second chance to make satisfying, mutually rewarding relationships with significant adults outside his immediate family.

During the years from twelve to seventeen a second weaning takes place from dependence on parents and on authority in general; simultaneously there is a search for other model figures. This offers the chance to any adult closely concerned with the care of adolescents to have a profound influence on their personal and intellectual development. This requires a willingness to offer a relationship which enables the child to learn more adequately what was denied him in earlier years.

The unloved, rejected adolescent has failed to learn to make satisfying relationships. Often too he has felt or has actually been rejected by the educational system which he in turn has rejected as being of little relevance to himself. Yet the need to earn his living, to become independent and to find some interpretation of life, however vague or simple, remains. It is a period of heightened emotional awareness and receptiveness, but also of increased insecurity because he is on the threshold of a new world. The more his parents and his teachers have failed him, the more distrustful of adults will he be. Once his trust has been won he will become much more demanding than youngsters of his age. So the task of rehabilitation is arduous, complex and slow.

The same applies to educational rehabilitation. Indeed, very considerable resistance needs to be overcome, stemming from his profound belief in the inevitability of failure. Allied to this is a rejection of an educational approach or materials which in his eyes appear 'childish'. There are now books and other equipment available which avoid this pitfall, and it may well be worth while to have a stock available in all residential homes catering for the older age groups.

As to tackling the adolescent's educational backwardness and the part played in this by the houseparents, similar considerations apply to those discussed for younger children. There are no ready guidelines — each youngster needs to be considered in the light of his background, his personality and the educational facilities available both at his school and in the residential community.

The Way Ahead

There has been comparatively little study of the language development and scholastic attainment of children living in residential care. My own series of studies of the relation between deprivation and education was prompted by the fact that teachers of such children thought that many of them showed serious learning problems at school.

The findings confirmed that their views were justified (Pringle, 1971). Hence, whatever additional help, provision or treatment are, or may in future be used to supplement residential care, houseparents will inevitably — like a child's own parents — shoulder the major responsibility for fostering emotional, intellectual and language development.

In the light of these recently recognized needs, priorities may have to be reconsidered. The maximum possible time should be devoted to talking to children, reading and telling them stories, encouraging them to make up and act simple plays about everyday occurrences, inviting them to relate anything that has happened during the day — all aimed at helping them to express their feelings, ideas and thoughts. Deprived children need this help far beyond the stage when it is normally required because so many of them have missed these experiences at the right time.

Quick results cannot be expected. If there is a slow growth in the child's capacity to use and enjoy language, then gradual improvement in intelligence, adjustment and educational progress is likely to follow. Mixed age groups in residential units may also help: younger children learn from and imitate older ones, while the latter can be encouraged to play with, talk and read to the little ones, ostensibly to help houseparents but at the same time improving their own power and desire for self-expression.

The term 'substitute care' tends to suggest that it is second best compared with parental care. If the aim is a pale imitation of ordinary family life, this must be so. However, there is evidence, both from Israel and Russia, that this need not be the case, even for very young children (Bronfenbrenner, 1970; Pincus, 1970). Rather than providing a substitute home, the aim should be to create a different environment which offers an alternative form of care with its own satisfactions and challenges. The term 'community living' was chosen by such pioneers as Leila Rendel some fifty years ago, and it is perhaps a tribute to their leadership that the residential establishments, envisaged in the 1969 Children Act, are to be called 'community homes'.

Several ideas are implicit in this concept. Perhaps the two most important ones are that true community living can be an alternative way of life, neither better nor worse, but just different. Secondly, that it must be involved in the larger community in which it finds itself, rather than be inward looking and self-sufficient. There are many ways in which such involvement can be fostered. Of particular relevance in relation to language development and scholastic progress is the contribution of young volunteers from secondary schools and colleges of education. These young people may be willing in the evenings and at weekends to give individual and intensive help to a child. Such a scheme, in addition to providing a valuable link with the outside community, would also foster greater understanding of the aims and practice of residential work.

In brief, my argument can be summarized as follows. First, that love is not enough in caring for hurt, unhappy and damaged children, though it is and always will remain, an essential ingredient. Secondly, that a knowledge of normal child development is a necessary basis for understanding the needs of deprived children. Thirdly, that houseparents need to add to their many other responsibilities a very specific concern for the language development and educational progress of the children in their care. Fourthly, that realistic yet positive standards of expectation are a vital ingredient in bringing about change. Fifthly, that the peer group has great re-educational and therapeutic value. And lastly, that though residential care is an alternative means of looking after children in a community setting, the houseparent will always be concerned with and for every child as an individual.

References

BLOOM, B.S. (1964) *Stability and Change in Human Characteristics*, Wiley and Sons, New York.

BRONFENBRENNER, U. (1970) *Two Worlds of Childhood, U.S.A. and U.S.S.R.*, Russell Sage Foundation, New York.

CRELLIN, E., PRINGLE, M.K. and WEST, P. (1971) *Born Illegitimate*, NFER, Slough.

DINNAGE, R. and PRINGLE, M.K. (1968) *Residential Care — Facts and Fallacies*, Longman in association with the National Children's Bureau, London.

DINNAGE, R. and PRINGLE, M.K. (1967) *Foster Care — Facts and Fallacies*, Longman in association with the National Children's Bureau, London.

DOUGLAS, J.W.B. (1964) *The Home and the School*, University of London Press.

MAPSTONE, E. (1969) 'Children in care', *Concern*, 3, National Children's Bureau, London.

PINCUS, C. (1970) *They Came from the Four Winds*, Herzl Press, New York.

PRINGLE, M.K. (1965, 2nd. ed. 1971) *Deprivation and Education*, Longman, London.

PRINGLE, M.K. (1966) *Adoption — Facts and Fallacies*, Longman in association with the National Children's Bureau, London.

PRINGLE, M.K. (Ed.) (1969) *Caring for Children*, Longman in association with the National Children's Bureau, London.

Chapter 7

The Educational Needs of Deprived Children*

The Problem

Listening to the comments of their teachers would lead one to think that deprived children have greater educational difficulties than those living in their own homes. Similarly, the remarks made by superintendents and house staff of children's homes suggest that they accept a disproportionate number of unfavourable school reports as a usual occurrence. This raises two questions: first, whether the incidence of educational difficulties is in fact higher among deprived than ordinary children; and second, whether this is inevitable.

Incidence of Backwardness and Retardation

A recent study carried out by one of my research students clearly shows that the problem of school failure is at least twice as serious for children in care. We took attainment in reading as a measure of educational achievement because this subject is the most basic educational skill. Particularly in the primary school, backwardness in reading has an adverse effect on a child's progress in most other work. Moreover, it is only for this subject that the extent of backwardness in the ordinary school population is known, so that a standard for comparison is available.

Before the second question can be answered, namely whether this greater backwardness found among deprived children is inevitable, the nature of educational difficulties needs to be considered. The term

*This paper was originally published in *Child Care*, 11, 1, January 1957, pp. 4–8, and subsequently in *Deprivation and Education*, Longman, 1965, (2nd ed. 1971).

'backward' tends to be used for a number of different conditions. First, dull children who suffer from limitations due to inborn factors and show all-round limited capacity to learn, are described as backward (IQ range approximately 70–85). Second, children who experience learning difficulties in school are usually called backward. But when educational achievement is taken as the criterion, two subgroups can be distinguished: first, the backward; and second, the retarded. The attainments of backward pupils are below the standard reached by the majority of their contemporaries by 15 per cent or more. Mentally dull backward children are inevitably backward educationally. Even when working up to capacity, dull children, by the very nature of their handicap, are unable to do as well as the majority of average intelligence.

Retarded or underfunctioning pupils fail to reach a level of educational attainment commensurate with their mental ability, i.e. their achievement falls seriously below the level of their capacity. Thus while in backwardness a child's attainments are compared with those of his contemporaries, in retardation a pupil's achievements are considered in relation to his own mental capacity.

Exact information regarding the proportions of dull children in the school population is not available, but estimates vary between 10 and 15 per cent. Even less information is available for deprived children, but the results of our work suggest that the incidence of mental dullness is at least twice as high among them. This higher proportion is not unexpected since children in care come predominantly from that section of the community which deals less adequately with the complex problems of modern life. Among the important causes for their inadequacy is limited intelligence. Therefore one would expect to find a greater number of dull children among the deprived than in a random section of the population. Because of this, a higher incidence of educational backwardness is inevitable.

In the ordinary population about 15 per cent are dull, 70 per cent are of average, and 15 per cent of very good intelligence. On the other hand, among deprived children we found only five of very good intelligence, 60 per cent in the average group, and 35 per cent who were dull. Nevertheless, the majority are of average intelligence just as in the ordinary population. This is of relevance when one considers the extent of educational retardation. Again quoting from my own research, twice to three times as many deprived children are retarded at the age of 11 years than is the case among ordinary children (the respective proportions being 35 per cent against 12 per cent). While mental dullness, and educational backwardness caused by it, is irremediable, most cases of educational retardation respond to remedial treatment. Clearly the need for such help is even more urgent for deprived children than for those living in their own homes.

A third aspect that has a bearing on educational needs is speech or language development. Other work has suggested that deprived children tend to be rather limited in this respect and we also found that, compared with normal children, they are severely limited in their capacity to understand and use their mother tongue. For example many eight-year-olds did not know the name for a safety-pin, razor blades, the plumber, the postman, nostrils and eyelashes.

Causes of Language and Educational Retardation

Why should deprived children be more retarded educationally and in language development than ordinary children? As in most psychological work, there is unlikely to be just one cause but rather a multiplicity of interacting and interdependent factors. In recent years the close link between emotional factors and learning in childhood has come to be recognized. To look only at the failing school child or only at his intellectual capacity does not get to the root of the trouble. Intellectual development — particularly in its early stages — depends on the existence of a satisfactory relationship with a loved adult whose approval and appreciation is needed for every small achievement. Thus a loving, educated and cultured home provides a sound foundation for success at school. Needless to say, few children in care come from such homes. Many have grown up in a family broken in spirit or in reality, or afflicted by mental illness; they have been moved around among relatives, institutions, and foster homes and have lacked a continuous, loving relationship with a mother or a mother substitute. The child whose early learning efforts met with little interest will now bring his apathetic, discouraged attitude into the classroom. Being emotionally insecure and having only a limited speaking vocabulary, educational difficulties are likely to follow. Moreover, a vicious circle is often set up on starting school. Because he is insecure and discouraged he fails to do as well as other children. The teacher, very understandably, is disappointed at a lack of response and progress, and this disapproval makes the deprived child feel yet more hopeless and apathetic.

The Meaning of Remedial Treatment

It must be stressed that this term is not synonymous with coaching. For the child who is otherwise well-adjusted in school and has a positive attitude to learning, intensive help with one particular subject may be sufficient. For seriously retarded children coaching is ineffective. In remedial teaching the problem is tackled on a wide front. Before teaching in the narrower sense of the word can be undertaken, it is essential to widen his horizon, broaden his interests, develop his power of self-expression, and stimulate his desire to talk and communicate. Moreover, severe educational failure is almost invariably accompanied by emotional difficulties, ranging from lack of concentration, day-dreaming, and apathy to aggressiveness, truancy and delinquency. Therefore, creative and therapeutic activities such as puppetry, miming, modelling, painting, sand and water play, are an essential part of remedial treatment. When successful, it results not only in considerable acceleration in the rate of educational progress, but more important, perhaps, children's attitudes to learning, to difficulties, and to challenge improve. This may also lead to a remission of symptoms such as aggressiveness or timidity.

Educationally retarded children require remedial treatment until they have caught up on the basic subjects and are able to succeed without special attention. Thus remedial help need be given for a limited period of time only, until the child is working approximately up to his mental level. It is of greatest benefit to children of average and above average ability, though underfunctioning dull children can also be helped. However, the latter tend to make slow progress unless daily help can be given. Dull children are best catered for in special classes (where the whole teaching programme can be adapted to their slower rate of learning) unless the ordinary classes are small enough for the teacher to devote individual attention to them.

Organization of Remedial Work

It would be best if a variety of schemes were tried: first, because there are different needs in different areas as well as differing facilities and resources; second, because different methods might be appropriate for short-term and long-term cases; and third, because there is need for experiment in a new field, such as this, to find suitable methods. Specially trained remedial teachers are, of course, best qualified to undertake this work, but if none are available it should be entrusted to experienced teachers who have special interest in this field. The most essential personal qualities needed are patience, an understanding of emotional difficulties and flexibility.

According to the size of a children's Home, one or two teachers might be employed full-time. Some children will arrive with detailed psychological and educational reports which will show whether remedial teaching is required before they attend ordinary schools. Others will need to be given a diagnostic examination before this decision can be made. According to the severity and nature of their difficulties they may either be given all their teaching in the home or, alternatively, receive special help for two or three periods during the week, otherwise attending school in the usual way. Children who are fostered out or who live in small family homes could also benefit by attending for remedial help either full- or part-time.

For short-term cases coming into care it might be argued that having to adjust to life in a children's Home and to a new school during a brief period of time is making things doubly difficult for a child who has already been an educational problem in his previous school. The time away from home might be made profitable for those who are seriously retarded by providing intensive remedial help instead of the children attending local schools.

If full-time teachers cannot be employed, either because of the cost or because of lack of premises or because the size of the problem does not warrant a full-time person, part-time teachers may be used to give children extra help after school hours, in the evenings or during the weekend. Such teachers could be peripatetic, calling at different residential Homes as well as visiting foster homes. An alternative, which would save the teacher's time, would be to have central premises to which the children could go.

Present Facilities

If it is accepted, for a variety of interacting conditions, the incidence of emotional difficulties and educational backwardness is higher among children in residential care than among the population at large, then more provision would seem to be necessary for the former. However, at present the opposite is the case. It is well known that there is a severe shortage of psychotherapeutic and remedial provision in the country as a whole, the more serious the further away northwards an area is from the Home Counties. Deprived children are doubly handicapped by being at a disadvantage regarding the availability of appropriate treatment: psychotherapy is usually provided less readily for them than for the child who lives with his own family on the grounds that the child guidance team must work with the parents in order fully to help the child; and that in any case, his emotional disturbance is to some considerable degree due to his deprivation. With regard to receiving remedial treatment for his educational backwardness, here too he has to compete for limited facilities. Again he is at a disadvantage because of his often low scores on verbal intelligence tests and because of his frequently apathetic attitude to school work; both these are considered contraindications to successful remedial results and so he is less likely to be selected for it.

Since remedial treatment has a stabilizing influence and enables children to fit in more happily at school, it seems even more urgent that it should be provided for deprived than for ordinary children. This leads to the thorny question of who should pay for it. To make adequate educational provision is of course the duty of Local Education Authorities and not of Children's Committees. However, only few authorities provide remedial facilities, due mainly to the shortage of teachers, buildings and finance. One may hopefully look forward to the day when all areas will have remedial treatment available for everyone who needs it, or, even more Utopian, to a time when classes will be so small that teachers can afford to give individual attention to all failing children. Meanwhile, it might be of interest to mention the facilities at present available specifically for deprived children.

When, two years ago, [i.e. in 1955] I first reported the results of our research regarding the educational needs of deprived children, the only remedial provision specifically available for them was an experiment begun by the Church of England Children's Society (and described by Dr A. Bowley in *Child Care*). Since then, partly as a result of our findings, three further schemes have been started, each organized and financed in a different way.

The Children's Officer of Birmingham, Mr E.J. Holmes, was successful in securing his Committee's consent to employing part-time remedial teachers. By this action a welcome precedent has been set. In the first place the scheme will run for a limited period, four trained remedial teachers carrying out the work in two larger Homes after school hours. Results achieved so far are encouraging, despite the fact that out-of-school work is not ideal, since both children and teachers are not at their best at the end of the day.

The second scheme owes its inspiration to the Superintendent of one of the larger L.C.C. Children's Homes. Having grown increasingly concerned about the children's educational difficulties and concomitant behaviour problems, he succeeded in gaining his Committee's support for a remedial unit to be established on the premises. This is staffed by a full-time teacher who is employed and paid by the Local Education Authority. Again, results achieved so far are reported to be satisfactory.

The third scheme owes its existence to the pioneering spirit and foresight of Miss Leila Rendel of the Caldecott Community, who decided to devote some research funds made available to her by the Nuffield Foundation to an experiment in this field. She hoped that if results proved satisfactory, they would stimulate the setting up of similar units and the development of remedial work for deprived children. The unit, consisting of two self-contained, fully equipped rooms (a classroom and a play room) is in charge of a fulltime, trained remedial teacher and children attend for varying periods according to their needs (from daily sessions to twice a week), while spending the rest of the day in their ordinary schools. Organized as a pilot research project, the methods of work used are closely similar to those developed at Birmingham University's Remedial Education Centre. Regular case conferences are held, attended by the teachers and house staff concerned, to discuss children's progress and to select new cases to be admitted to the unit. Very detailed records and test results are being kept so that a full evaluation can be made at the end of two years.

It might be of interest to mention briefly the progress made by a boy who has attended this unit for only four months. Billy was referred by the Children's Officer for serious difficulties at school; both his work and behaviour were stated to be 'appallingly poor'. Billy's story is not untypical of children in care: an illegitimate child of a rather feckless young woman, he had been placed in a children's Home at the age of eighteen months. His mother kept up a spasmodic contact, making extravagant promises of taking him home, when in fact she has never had one, being either in resident-work or living 'with a friend'. By the age of eight he had been to four different homes and three different schools. He was then befriended, through the 'Uncle and Aunt Scheme', by a couple who had two children of their own and who eventually offered to accept him as a foster child. As was to be expected, there were a number of crises, when it looked as if the arrangement would break down, but now a year and a half later Billy was settled happily with them, except that his foster mother was very concerned about his lack of educational attainments, because his reports stated with monotonous regularity that 'he does not concentrate and shows no interest in his work. A slow child who could, however, do much better than this.' His foster parents had tried to help him. This was not a success as he seemed to resent it, and became surly and stubborn. At first this attitude also characterized his manner when he began to attend the remedial unit. Though aged nine and a half, he had hardly made a start with reading and his achievement in arithmetic was only slightly better. Contrary to his school reports he was found to be of average intelligence (I.Q. 90) and not mentally dull. At first his behaviour was similar to that shown at school: he bullied other children, lacked concentration, was sullen in his attitude to the remedial teacher and resented any direct suggestions. No teaching was attempted during the first few sessions (he attended once a week for two hours together with three other boys), but his play activities clearly showed his need to explore all available media. Gradually his attitude to the remedial teacher changed and not only did he greatly look forward to his visits, but he began to talk freely and spontaneously and to accept suggestions from her. Having explored his interest, prereading activities were introduced in the form of games which eventually led to the making of his own illustrated reading book and to keeping a simple diary in coop-eration with the other boys. Though at the end of his first term's attendance no measurable or testable improvement in attainments had taken place, his attitude to learning and to being taught had become considerably modified. He is likely to respond next term to a more formal and systematic approach to reading in the first place, and later to the other basic subjects. Mean-while, some improvement in behaviour has been reported by his school.

Present Needs

Great strides have been made since the passing of the Children Act in almost every aspect except the educational field. There is an urgent need for remedial treatment among children in care and little hope, at least for the near future, that Local Education Authorities will be able to make the necessary provision. It is therefore suggested that as a temporary emergency measure Children's Committees accept responsibility for making such help available and, if necessary, pay for it. At the same time they should, as ordinary parents can and do, continue to bring the seriousness of the problem to the notice of the Local Authority and press for remedial facilities to be made available at the earliest opportunity.

Some help can also be given by housemothers and foster parents. As much time as possible should be devoted to talking to the children, reading and telling them stories, getting them to make up and act simple plays about everyday occurrences, encouraging them to relate small happenings that take place during the day to express their feelings, ideas and thoughts. This kind of help needs to be given to most deprived children much longer than is usual, because so often they have missed these experiences at the right time. Quick returns can therefore not be expected, but if there is a slow growth in their capacity to enjoy and use language, there is likely to follow also an improvement in adjustment both in the Home and at school. With children under school age such activities can be regarded as preventive. The system of family units, which is being increasingly introduced into Children's Homes, may also help to foster language development among all ages; the younger ones will learn from and imitate the older, while the older children can be encouraged to read and talk to the little ones, ostensibly to help houseparents and the family unity, but in fact also improving their own power and wish for self-expression.

Chapter 8

Better Adoption*

In 1946, the Curtis committee recommended adoption as the best form of substitute care. This view was based on a belief in the value of family life rather than on any evidence. Now, a quarter of a century later, this belief has been vindicated by our National Children's Bureau study, *Growing Up Adopted*. This reports the findings of the first longitudinal investigation of a nationally representative group of adopted children and their families ever carried out in Britain.

The nature of the data obtained by the National Children's Bureau made it possible to compare — both at birth and at the age of seven — the whole child population and those who are subsequently adopted. (Figure 1 shows trends in adoption.) Comparisons were also made between those illegitimately born children who were being brought up by their own mothers and those who were adopted (Figure 2, from the earlier study, *Born Illegitimate*, gives one kind of comparison).

Our evidence, as well as that of others, suggests that adoption is the best form of substitute care yet devised by our society, for children whose parents are unable, unwilling or unfit to provide a suitable and permanent home for them. Best, if for no other reason (and there *are* other reasons), because it has a far lower failure rate than residential or foster care; and because the adopted children did so well that they are indistinguishable from the population at large — in contrast to other children deprived of living with their natural parents.

As in so many other fields, there are 'fashions' in child care. It used to be thought that because a child is upset when a parent has to leave after visiting him in a children's home or foster home, it might be wiser or kinder for such visits to be infrequent. Also, it was too readily assumed that a

*Following publication of the research study *Growing Up Adopted*, NFER, 1972, this article appeared in *New Society*, 20, 509, 29 June, 1972, pp. 676–8.

parent who did not visit had ceased to care for the child. It was subsequently argued that even if meetings were painful for both sides, to maintain contact was of great importance to the child and everything should be done to help the parent do so.

Now the pendulum seems to have swung too far, so that it is held that even a 'bad' and neglectful parent is better than any kind of substitute care. Hence, every means of persuasion should be tried to make the parent visit or take the child back home. In truth, though the great majority of parents care for their children, some do not, or are incapable of it. Therefore, prevention and rehabilitation must be employed with discrimination, judgement and realism.

Moreover, it seems totally unjustifiable to use a child as a therapeutic agent for his parents — whether they are his natural parents, but so immature, inadequate or disturbed themselves that it will be a very long term process to rehabilitate them; or whether they are adoptive parents, who hope that their unsatisfactory marriage will be improved by having a baby.

It follows, then, that it is as wrong to give a child to an adoptive mother, merely because she can provide all physical comforts, as it is to persuade a mother to keep her illegitimate baby merely because she has given birth to it; or to take a child back home who has been in care, when it is necessary to keep trying to stimulate a parent's faint and intermittent flicker of interest in him. It is over such children that one advocates a loss of parental rights. Their number is likely to be not inconsiderable since a recent inquiry showed that over half the children in foster homes had been apart from their own families for five years or more; a proportion of these would undoubtedly be children whose parents rarely visit or write.

When conflicts arise between the rights of parents and those of children, they are still most often resolved in favour of the former. Current legislation is based on the Adoption Act, 1958. It, too, did not make the welfare of the child paramount, or even as important as the rights of the parents. The act, did, however, introduce a new provision under which a parent's consent could be dispensed with, if the court was satisfied that the parent had persistently failed, without reasonable cause, to discharge his parental obligations.

Though this provision made possible the adoption of children deprived of adequate parental care, in practice it has hardly been used. Among the most likely reasons is that the rights and interests of parents — whether natural or adoptive — continue to be regarded as more important than those of the child.

It is to be hoped that the departmental committee which is now reviewing adoption will recommend that 'the principle of the long-term

Fig 1: Adoptions in Great Britain

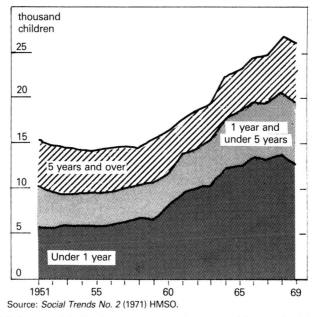

Source: *Social Trends No. 2* (1971) HMSO.

Fig 2: Children with 'below average' general knowledge
(Teachers' ratings)

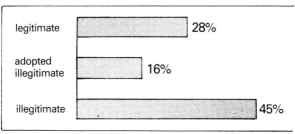

Source: *Born Illegitimate,* National Childrens Bureau.

welfare of the child should be the first and paramount consideration in adoption law,' as was suggested in its working paper. Making the child the focus — both when considering whether the family circumstances are such that he should be relinquished for this particular form of substitute care and when selecting adoptive parents — will require the establishment of new criteria and new methods, both in family case work, and in adoption policy and practice.

Traditional adoption procedures also need to be challenged in the light of established knowledge about the needs and development of children. Of the many current practices which our research questions, only three are considered here: the selection of babies 'suitable' for adoption; 'matching' the child and his adoptive parents; and the selection of prospective adopters.

The decision to adopt is based, broadly speaking, on one of two wishes: either to have a child, which the couple is unable to produce themselves, in which case they are likely to hope for a 'perfect baby', just as ordinary parents do; or it is based predominantly on the wish to provide a loving home for a child in need of it. The first group ought to be helped to realize that their desire cannot be met for two reasons: first because 'perfect' babies are in short supply and are likely to become even scarcer; secondly, because the younger the baby the less possible to forecast with any accuracy his likely future development.

As our research shows, advantage lies with early placement, except for the need of the biological mother for sufficient time to reach a firm decision. Yet developmental tests, administered during early infancy, have very limited predictive validity. Moreover, a study by L. Ripple in 1968 revealed that children for whom some minor difficulties were noted in the pre-adoptive or supervision periods, were less likely to show problems at follow-up than were children for whom no difficulties at all had been noted.

'Matching' for similarities in physical appearance, temperament or intelligence, is yet another myth which needs to be abandoned. Having been led to expect similarities between their adopted children and themselves, adoptive parents will feel cheated and justifiably resentful if their expectations are subsequently not fulfilled.

But perhaps most important of all, none of Ripple's evidence showed matching to be a favourable factor. 'The only associations, in fact, were in the opposite direction. Families in the "very high" match group on physical resemblance and ethnic background had more children in the problem groups at follow-up, and those in the "very low" match group had fewer children showing problems.' In addition, there is evidence from the work reported in the 1960s by Skodak, Skeels and Witmer that children from a very unpromising background placed into adoptive homes of a much superior level, tend to develop intellectual abilities more closely in keeping with those of their adoptive parents.

Thus there is little support for the current practice of placing children from the most favourable background in homes with the best 'apparent' potential, and those with the poorest history in homes with less obvious potential. If anything, the opposite would make more sense: the child whose background history has been the most favourable is likely to do well given a reasonably good home; the child who has been deprived, ill-treated, rejected, or who is handicapped or damaged in some other way, needs positive discrimination — i.e., the best possible environment — if he is to recover. Recent research has shown the remarkable extent to which this is possible — even for children adopted late (aged between five and eleven years) and after prolonged deprivation in early life.

Just as hazardous as 'matching' is the attempt to make long-term predictions about adoptive parenthood. Couples who are obviously unsuitable can be detected, but the more intelligent, educated and informed they are, the more likely it is that they will know how to present themselves in the most favourable light. This may be one reason why higher educational and economic status have been shown by several follow-up studies to be less favourable in relation to long-term outcome. So what is the alternative?

To begin with, selection should be replaced by self-evaluation and by preparation. Since nature has arranged for a nine-month waiting and preparatory time, might a similar period be considered appropriate? Instead of the prolonged process of investigation, the primary aim would be to achieve self-selection.

Perhaps the simplest way of determining whether a couple's basic motivation is to provide a good home for a child who needs it, would be to stipulate that, from now on, prospective adopters can no longer make stipulations. After all, this merely puts them on a par with biological parents; they, too, are not able to determine beforehand the sex, appearance, intelligence or health of their child.

The risk of having a child who is seriously handicapped, mentally or physically, is less than the risk of subsequent injury in an accident. Two exceptions might be made: first, parents would be able to choose whether they wish to have a child whose skin is the same colour as their own since this is also within the control of natural parents. Second, severely disabled and grossly deformed babies would not be made available for adoption.

No doubt some couples would not even apply for a child, once this condition of 'no stipulation' has been laid down. For the others the preparatory period would have four broad aims. The first would be to give an understanding of normal child development, with particular stress on the preschool period.

Secondly, it would be frankly admitted that few, if any, of the children available for adoption are 'as good as new'; to a greater or lesser extent most of them will have been exposed to some unfavourable early influences, such as a stressful pregnancy, late ante-natal care, an unsettled early life, and so on. To that extent, adoptive parents have to be prepared to take greater risks than ordinary parents.

Thirdly, prospective adopters would be given the opportunity to learn from established adoptive parents about the joys and difficulties specific to adoption. And last, but by no means least, adopters should be given the most recent knowledge there is about the influence and relevance of heredity and environment; above all, they need to understand the positive power of optimistic (but not over-ambitious) expectations and the danger of pessimistic, self-fulfilling prophecies. The fact that all studies of adopted children have shown that the kind of home parents provide and the kind of care they bestow are the most important preconditions for a satisfactory outcome, needs to be stressed again and again, to dispel deep-seated yet unjustified fears of the effects of poor heredity.

If a child suffers from a physical defect or disability, then the adoptive parents should, of course, be told about it in the same way as all parents have the right to expect to be told. Whether or not adoptive parents should be given some priority in the allocation of diagnostic treatment and educational services is an open question. On the one hand, it could be argued that they perform a social service in accepting as their own a child who has special needs. On the other hand, if it is accepted that adoptive parenthood should be recognized not as a second-best but as an alternative to 'biological' parenting, then it might be better not to give any preferential treatment.

We know enough for policy and practice to be changed so that couples come to the fore who have the greatest potential for becoming 'ideal adopters'. These would be the couples who take the child as they have taken each other, for better for worse.

References

CRELLIN, E., PRINGLE, M.K. and WEST, P. (1971) *Born Illegitimate: Social and Educational Implications*, NFER.

KADUSHIN, K. (1970) *Adopting Older Children*, New York, Columbia University Press.

LAKER, C.A. and TONGUE, I.M. (1971) 'New rights for foster parents: An exploratory study of the departmental committee's proposals concerning foster parents' future rights to apply for adoption or guardianship, and of the views of professional staff concerning these proposals', *Concern*, 8, pp. 19–25.

RIPPLE, L. (1968) 'A follow-up study of adopted children', *Social Service Review*, 4, 42, pp. 479–99.

SKEELS, H.M. (1965) 'Effects of adoption on children from institutions', *Children*, 12, pp. 33–4.

SKODAK, M. and SKEELS, H.M. (1949) 'A final follow-up study of one hundred adopted children', *Journal of Genetic Psychology*, 75, pp. 85–125.

WITMER, H.L., HERZOG, E., WEINSTEIN, E.A. and SULLIVAN, M.E. (1963) *Independent Adoptions — A Follow-up Study*, New York, Russell Sage Foundation.

Chapter 9

Whither Residential Child Care?*

Research evidence shows that life in institutions has damaging effects on the inmates. This is true whether they are adult prisoners, borstal boys, mental hospital patients, or children in residential care or long-stay hospitals. The younger the 'inmate', the more harmful the consequences for emotional, intellectual and educational development are likely to be. First, and perhaps more lasting and pervasive, is the loss of a sense of identity. There are three basic questions to which, all too often, the child receives no answer: Who am I? Why am I here? And where am I going? Not only does the child in long-term care have no reliable past; equally devastating, he has no predictable future, except that he will come out of care at the age of eighteen. Often he is uncertain why he came into care; why changes in his placements were made; why other children moved on; and why staff left. Often he does not know or has no means of remembering the full names of the various people who have looked after him, let alone their current whereabouts; the same is true regarding the children who shared his life for certain periods. He does not know what his future is likely to hold, since long-term plans are rarely made; and if made, they are neither discussed with nor divulged to him.

The constantly shifting population militates against establishing dependable and lasting relationships, either with staff or other children. All too often previous relationships with parents, members of the extended family, school friends and children in the neighbourhood have also become tenuous, if not broken altogether. Another ill effect is loss of privacy and the surrender of individuality. Last, but by no means least, children in residential homes have to bear a stigma which is no less painful for being irrational. Though the vast majority are there because of family breakdown, they are made to feel guilty of some wrongdoing. Whether the designation of approved schools as community homes has increased this

*First published in *Concern*, 26, 1977–8, pp. 5–10.

stigma, is an open question. Or perhaps it is inherent in a system which uses the term 'care' for something that is imposed on those who receive it.

What Has Changed in the Past Decade?

Regrettably, very little has changed in the past decade. Even the number of children in care has not been reduced. It now stands over 120,000 and numbers are still rising. This despite the more community-orientated philosophy that was enshrined in the 1969 Children and Young Persons Act. Nor is it for lack of knowledge, although more needs to be found out. Ten years ago the Bureau published *Residential Child Care — Facts and Fallacies*[1], a review of what was known then, both in this country and abroad. We concluded that 'the picture is not an encouraging one for those who would want the child entrusted to public care, to have as nearly as possible the same opportunities as the average child will have in his own family'. But when ten years later the Bureau updated the previous literature review, the sad conclusion was: 'Very little appeared to have changed, either in the nature of residential care itself in this country or in the findings of research which could themselves inform policy and practice . . . While legislative changes appear to have inflated the number of children who are in care, there is still a real underlying increase over time, even where allowance is made for these changes'[2].

Some changes there have been. Ten years on from 1966, the number of children in residential care has practically doubled, although this includes some 15,000 previously in approved schools. The proportion admitted to care on a short-term basis has, however, decreased from about 50 per cent to 30 per cent. The principal reasons for admission of children who remain in long-term care include abandonment; mother's death or desertion; parental long-term illness, particularly mental illness; and committal under a Fit Person Order. A substantial proportion of those in long-term care are illegitimate or coloured or are handicapped — physically, emotionally or both; and many have less than average educational attainments.

There is some new evidence too in relation to coloured children in long-term care. Only a minority come from normal intact families, fewer than one child in five having lived with both parents. Research has also dispelled certain myths which have common currency at present: such as that coloured children are new immigrants who come into care soon after arriving in this country because of 'culture shock'; or that coloured families break down because the parent-child bond has been weakened by separation in consequence of parents arriving years in advance of their children and then sending for them later. In fact, the majority of coloured children in care were born in the UK; and the great majority of their immigrant parents have lived in the country for at least two years prior to the child's admission to care.

What Has Not Changed in Residential Care?

The short answer to this question is: the likely emotional, intellectual and educational consequences; and hence the long-term psychological ill-effects and social costs, both to the children and then later to the community at large. Prolonged institutionalization during the early years of life leaves children very vulnerable to later stress; there is no new evidence which contradicts this conclusion. On the contrary, both language and intellectual retardation become the more serious, the less adequate the psychological care. Among children of school age, lower levels of language, intellectual and educational performance have been found in studies both in this country and elsewhere. These findings have been confirmed by the Bureau's National Child Development Study. The proportion performing poorly in general knowledge, ability to express themselves in conversation, reading and arithmetic, was twice or three times as high among children 'in care' as among their peers. Hence, as expected, a proportionately large number were thought to need special educational help.

The Proper Role for Residential Care

In my view, institutions should not be expected to provide substitute parental care either on a short- or a long-term basis. Neither should they be considered suitable placements for children while appropriate long-term plans are being worked out; nor, worst of all, as a 'last resort' because no other alternatives are available or have not yet produced the desired results. Instead they must be given a positive and well defined role. No service can develop high standards and maintain good morale if it appears to have only a kind of all-purpose 'dustbin' function.

What then should this role be? I see it as being parallel to that of special schools in the educational, and hospitals in the health field; places where special knowledge and skills are employed to remedy or at least ameliorate appropriately diagnosed needs. Just as hospitals and special schools now aim to return patients or pupils to their own homes or ordinary schools at the earliest possible time, so residential care would aim to enable children to return to ordinary family life, whether with their own or substitute parents.

If this concept of residential care were to be accepted, then it would have two main functions, both of them constructive and positive. The first task would be relatively subsidiary and short-term, namely to carry out a full assessment. Only under special circumstances need assessment be undertaken residentially — a useful analogy being admission to hospital for observation and tests.

The second and major task of residential care would be the rehabilitation and treatment of children and young people, too disturbed or damaged to cope with ordinary family life. This would include those who are a danger to themselves or others, and hence require a sheltered and secure environment for a period of time. But for them too, the long-term aim would be to return them to normal family living. If there is no viable family, then it would be essential to provide a substitute family, even for a young adult. To return him to life in the community without a supportive family base is to make reintegration much more taxing and hazardous.

To fulfil this major task, institutions for children must become therapeutic communities, staffed by highly trained, experienced workers. Because of the very demanding, complex nature of their job, they would require the support of advisers and consultants, including psychiatrists, psychotherapists, psychologists, paediatricians and remedial teachers. Instead of being the Cinderella among social services staff, they would become highly specialized key workers, requiring training additional to that of field social workers.

Therapeutic communities attempt to find answers to a whole range of questions for each individual child, such as: in what areas of development are compensatory or therapeutic experiences most urgently needed? How are these to be provided? By whom and for how long? When is an individual and when a group approach more appropriate? What should be the aim of enrichment programmes at different ages? What are the role and function of educational remedial work? How can a child best be helped to understand and come to terms with his past, including inadequate, rejecting or cruel parents? In short, what must be done for each child so that he leaves residential care emotionally and intellectually strengthened — if not healed and restored — rather than even more deficient or damaged than when he entered it?

A Ten Point Plan for a Ten-Year Programme

'Community care' is now a fashionable concept which has become increasingly attractive politically since it is being seen as a far less costly alternative to residential care. However, if the community is not willing to care, then community care is doomed to remain an empty slogan. The acid test of this willingness could well be children. After all, the young should arouse both compassion and sympathy more readily than the old, the mentally ill, the physically handicapped, drug addicts, alcoholics, or any other groups for whom community care is advocated nowadays.

The cost of residential child care is extremely high. It ranges from a minimum of £2000 to £20,000 per annum per place for the different types of provision, excluding capital costs. Therefore a reduction in the number of children coming into residential care would represent a substantial saving which could be diverted into preventive and community-based facilities. It would not be realistic, however, to expect any reductions in the average cost per child in residential care; if anything, the contrary would happen.

To begin with, the training essential for residential staff is bound to be costly. Next, in order to undertake rehabilitation and therapy, each member of staff could be responsible only for a small number of children. Further, the more effective preventive measures and community placements become, the more difficult, disturbed and damaged would be the children needing residential care; hence short-term stays would tend to be the exception rather than the rule.

It is, of course, unrealistic to expect quick or drastic changes. But a real will to bring about change could transform the child care scene within ten years since sufficient knowledge has existed and been documented for the past twenty years at least. The ten point plan suggested below is designed both to reduce the number of children in residential care and at the same time to improve its quality. Some of the suggestions outlined are then discussed in greater detail in the papers which follow.

1   *Preventive measures.* Large families with low income, one-parent families and those where there is chronic physical or mental handicap, are at highest risk of disintegration. Once the family unit is broken, reintegration becomes more difficult. Hence, greatly improved child benefits for all families; special allowances for single parents; a greatly increased home help service; a corps of peripatetic housemothers; more day foster care for under-fives as well as older children; expanded day care facilities, making use of the plant of schools and residential homes; all these have a contribution to make. This does not, however, imply that *any* family is better than a substitute family nor that retaining a child within its biological family must *always* be the overriding aim.

2   *An early warning and support system.* An integrated service for children and their families should operate an early warning system. For example, research shows that the first occasion when a child's removal from home has to be considered should in fact be regarded as a danger signal of his being 'at

risk', i.e. living in an environment which is to some extent inadequate. Hence immediate help is needed to strengthen the family as well as continuing surveillance of the child's development and progress.

Long-term social work support — of the type given by Family Service Units — for emotionally immature or inadequate parents who nevertheless love their children, may succeed in keeping the family together. Compensatory preschool measures could given the intellectual and social stimulation lacking in such homes. For older children, remedial help should be provided as well as supervised adventure playgrounds, clubs and holiday camps. These are just some of the measures which could widen vulnerable children's horizons and keep them constructively occupied during weekends and holidays.

3 *Greatly increased intermediate treatment facilities offering a wide spectrum of options.*

4 *Much earlier and much better planning for children having to be received into care.*

5 *Reducing the stigma of care.* If the community is to become more involved, a more realistic understanding of why children are received into care will have to be achieved. The current public image is of children who are either orphans or who have been in trouble of one kind or another. In the vast majority of cases, neither is true.

6 *Increasing the number of foster parents.* To overcome the accumulated backlog of children remaining in residential care, a concentrated and co-ordinated effort is imperative. A much more flexible and bigger pool of foster homes than exists at present needs to be developed: some to undertake short-term emergency fostering; some to work closely with the social work agency and the child's parents, even if the placement is likely to be long-term; some to specialize in caring for babies, the handicapped, or delinquent children; and some to provide a permanent home, becoming a substitute family in the fullest sense of the term.

The practice of making fostering a salaried, and in a proportion of cases a professional, job is reported to operate successfully in Holland. In this country a number of pilot schemes are proving the feasibility of such ventures. The danger of exploitation and wrong motivation undeniably exists; inadequate or even no remuneration is, however, no guarantee against either. Nor are affection and payment mutually exclusive. Indeed, love alone is not enough in caring for someone else's unhappy, disturbed, if not damaged, child. There may well be a hitherto untapped pool of social workers, teachers and nurses who on marriage would prefer to undertake fostering in their own homes rather than go out to work, especially if they have children of their own.

7 *Training for residential staff.* This would be quite essential if they are to

undertake the new role envisaged for them. No longer would they be seen as parent substitutes but rather as fully trained, professional workers possessing therapeutic skills of a high order. A thorough knowledge of normal child development would be basic, added to which would be an understanding of the causes, meaning and manifestations of emotional disturbance and learning difficulties. These would provide the backcloth for acquiring the skills needed to create a therapeutic daily milieu as well as a rehabilitative programme tailored to each child's needs.

8   *Basic ground rules for residential staff*. Because of the very taxing nature of the work, no-one should remain in it for more than five to six years at a time. This would provide sufficient continuity since the great majority of children should not remain in residential care for more than three years. Staff would then be able to return to the normal pattern of professional life, i.e. not living in and through their work. It should be fully recognized for promotion within the social services career structure. Needless to say, residential workers would have to shoulder much more responsibility than at present for the care, assessment, treatment, forward planning and eventual transition of their charges into the outside world. A professional code of conduct and a contract outlining the expectations, rights and responsibilities of staff and children are ideas worth exploring.

9   *Supportive adults outside the residential community*. A new lease of life should be given to the 'uncle and aunt scheme', perhaps renaming it more appropriately. It would capitalize on the compassion and goodwill towards children among people who are unable or not yet ready to undertake fostering. It enables a child to have contact with ordinary family life and can lead to a continuing relationship, even if return to his own home is the long-term goal. Also, it provides a halfway house to full integration into the community.[3]

10   *The basic rights of children in care*. These must include the right to know their own family background; to be given a sense of continuity in their lives provided by photographs, letters, diaries and the like; to be consulted and involved in decisions affecting their future; and the right to privacy. These and many more have been fully spelt out by young people themselves in *Who Cares?*[4].

Recently an even more radical change has been suggested, namely that residential units be expanded and developed into community resource centres[5]. Again there is a parallel in the educational field, the proposal being that residential schools for handicapped children should perform a similar function. This new concept is not discussed here since it is unlikely to be translated into practice within the next ten years, even if pilot schemes were to demonstrate its feasibility.

References

1 DINNAGE, R. and PRINGLE, M.K. (1966) *Residential Child Care — Facts and Fallacies*, Longman in association with National Children's Bureau.
2 PROSSER, H. (1976) *Perspectives on Residential Child Care*, NFER for National Children's Bureau.
3 PRINGLE, M.K. (1971) *Deprivation and Education*, Longman in association with National Children's Bureau.
4 PAGE, R. and CLARK, G.A. (Eds) (1977) *Who Cares?* National Children's Bureau.
5 WARD, L. (1977) 'The Centre way to caring', *Community Care*, 5 October, pp. 18–20.

Chapter 10

A Ten Point Plan for Foster Care*

Fostering is becoming the preferred type of substitute care for children whose families cannot look after them temporarily or permanently, because it offers the closest approximation to normal family living, other than adoption. Consequently an increasing amount of professional skill, time and money is being devoted to it as well as to special innovatory schemes.

Hence it is urgent to explore how satisfactorily foster care is working both in the short and in the long run; how it may be improved; and whether some of its basic premises and principles require reconsideration. As a contribution to this rethinking, I am proposing a ten point plan. It aims both to reduce the number of children having to be separated from their own families and to improve the quality of foster care.

1   Preventive measures

Many children would never have to be admitted into care, if really adequate support services were available. To be effective, they must be comprehensive and integrated which requires greatly improved coordination between social, health and education services. Among the measures needed are much higher child benefits for all families; special allowances for single parents and those who care for a handicapped child; a greatly increased home help service including peripatetic housemothers; and day foster care for under-fives as well as older children.

2   An early warning and support system

Only an integrated service can operate such a system. For example, research shows that the first occasion when a child's removal from home becomes necessary is an early indication that he is 'at risk', i.e. living in an inadequate environment. Hence immediate help is needed to support, and if possible to

*First published in *Concern*, 30, 1978, pp. 5–10.

strengthen, the family as well as to monitor the child's subsequent development and progress.

Temporary placement in a day foster home could be part of such a
support system. It would avoid institutional care, as well as enable a full
assessment of the child's needs to be made in the atmosphere of an ordinary
family home.

3 Basic training in child development

This should be available to all prospective foster parents. While the capacity
to offer loving care is an essential prerequisite, love alone is not enough
when looking after someone else's unhappy, disturbed, if not damaged
child.

Knowledge of the needs of children and of the likely consequences
when some or all of them remain unmet, is vital to successful foster care. An
awareness of the causes, meaning and manifestations of emotional
disturbance and of learning difficulties would provide the basis for
developing the skills required to create a therapeutic, caring milieu as well
as a rehabilitative programme tailored to each child's needs.

Vital too is an appreciation of why it helps children to understand the
purpose of foster care and the reasons for their placement. Though these
may be deeply distressing, knowing the truth is less harmful than living in a
depersonalized vacuum, created by passive silence or by active conceal-
ment, or being haunted by fearful fantasies even more devastating than the
facts. Every child must be given as full an explanation as possible, and as is
within his understanding. This should not be a once-and-for-all occasion,
but become part of the process of maturation itself so that often repeated
information leads to an understanding and acceptance of his own past.

4 Selecting and preparing foster parents

Though recruitment, assessment and selection of foster homes are vital for
the success of placements, they have rarely been evaluated.

Are there still relatively untapped areas for recruitment? One such
could be ex-foster children who have established a satisfactory family life,
with children of their own; they may have something of special value to
offer based on their own experiences. Another potential source could be
couples with experience in relevant professional work, such as teaching,
health visiting, social work, etc. Some of the new Family Placement
Projects are recruiting such people.

In the absence of reliable criteria for recruiting and assessing foster
parents, might self-selection through a systematically planned process of
preparation and training be a better alternative? The majority may be
helped to decide for themselves whether they feel able to undertake this

task. Sensitive support should enable unsuitable couples to withdraw of their own accord without feelings of hurt and rejection.

Unrealistic expectations should be dispelled at the outset by a clear exposition why few of the children requiring fostering are 'as good as new'. Most will have suffered stressful experiences ranging from interrupted and multiple mothering to neglect and abuse, both physical and emotional. Hence prospective foster parents must be prepared to cope with greater problems and risks than ordinary parents. Successful foster parents could well teach about both the likely challenges and joys.

'Matching' children with foster parents seems an almost impossible undertaking: first, the former's unhappy experiences and consequent developmental problems, make it difficult to assess a child's 'real' personality; secondly, it is impossible to predict what changes in behaviour may occur if and when a child becomes able to respond fully to caring, consistent and dependable parenting. Almost incredible improvements do occur once a hitherto unloved child comes to accept that he is being loved and hence lovable; this enables him to learn to trust and love others in turn. Believing that basic changes are possible is half the battle.

Group methods of preparation are supplementary rather than an alternative to individual discussions and counselling. Also continuous support should be available to foster parents, particularly during the early period of a placement, supplemented by group meetings with other foster parents. Thus self-selection, preparation, training, subsequent casework and group support should be seen as interlinked and continuous processes.

5   *The issue of payment*

Whether a salary should be paid rather than only allowances for costs incurred, has for long been a controversial issue. That the danger of exploitation and wrong motivation exists is undeniable. Yet inadequate or even no remuneration are no guarantee against either; nor are affection and payment mutually exclusive.

The idea that fostering should not be done for financial reward belongs to an era when most workers in the helping professions were paid a pittance, partly on the grounds that it was a satisfying vocation. Now that nurses, teachers and social workers receive more adequate pay, no one claims that as a result they exploit those they care for. After marriage, some women in these professions may prefer to undertake fostering in their own homes rather than work outside, especially if they have young children. Adequate pay could be an added incentive.

An immediate step should be an agreed national minimum fostering allowance, linked thereafter to the cost of living. This would at least eradicate present inequalities. Next, the present rather small scale experiments should be followed by larger scale studies to compare the effects of fostering as a form of voluntary service, expenses only being paid. It should be preceded by a well designed recruiting campaign covering women's institutes, the church organizations, offices, factories and supermarkets, supplemented by articles in the local press, radio and television. Only in this way can the likely consequences of injecting a degree of professionalism into fostering be properly evaluated.

The Netherlands and Denmark (Bowen, 1969) operate a policy of realistic payments and foster homes are of a very high standard. In Holland excellent housing facilities and domestic help are provided. In Sweden, about 80 per cent of children in care are fostered.

6 *Differentiating between different fostering tasks*

Just as teachers and social workers have the opportunity for specialization, so some differentiation and choice for foster parents may lead to improvements. At least four different types might be distinguished.

Short-term or temporary care: this would encompass emergency placements due to unforeseen crises in the child's home; or a period of assessment to enable long-term plans to be made; or weekend as well as holiday stays for handicapped children whose parents need a respite; or similar periods for children living in institutional care who would benefit from having at least brief experiences of family life. The last mentioned would be akin to the 'uncle and aunt scheme' operated over twenty years ago with measurable success in promoting children's emotional adjustment and educational achievement (Pringle, 1971).

Day care for under fives might also be included, replacing the rather objectionable description of 'childminder' by the more appropriate one of day foster mother.

Children with special needs: among them are the severely disturbed emotionally; the physically and/or mentally handicapped; grossly neglected and abused children; and those showing delinquent behaviour. Included too should be children who have spent many years in institutional care, whose number would radically decline if residential care were to be replaced by foster care at a quicker rate than at present.

Fostering mixed age groups: combining different age groups, such as babies and adolescents, or children and old people, is considered an enriching and mutually supportive combination by some foster parents. Older adults, even if handicapped by physical disabilities, can provide a grandparent figure so often missing these days from the life of young people.

Long-term substitute parental care: intended for children unlikely to be returned to live with their own parents, this type of foster care comes nearest to adoption.

Some couples may choose and be able to undertake all four types of foster care, either simultaneously or at different times during their foster care career. However, most are likely to prefer one or other of these tasks.

It seems unwise to create two categories of foster parents, especially if one is regarded as superior. This is implied by calling one group 'professional' foster care workers (or some such special designation) and the other 'traditional' foster parents. To pay an additional special responsibility allowance seems justified if additional, more lengthy training were demanded from those willing to accept short-term placements and children with special needs; also it would compensate for the fact that both these groups are more disruptive of the foster families' life and make greater demands in terms of time and adaptability.

7   Relationships between social workers and foster parents

Exercising quality control and providing support to foster parents must be accepted as an essential aspect of social work. This includes sharing information both about the child's past and future plans. Foster parents should by right be able to participate in the regular six monthly reviews and in the making of decisions affecting the child's life.

When a child has to leave a foster home, there should never be a complete break in contact, whether or not he returns to his own parents. At a minimum, to keep some link with people who have cared for him contributes to the child's memory store of personal relationships. In some cases this contact may come to provide a future lifeline in time of need.

8   Removing the stigma of care

The main reasons why children come into care are the illness of the parent or guardian; their own need for care and protection because of unsatisfactory home conditions; or because they have been deserted by one or both parents. Clearly all such events are totally outside the child's control. Yet many are left at the mercy of half-understood facts and unjustified feelings of guilt, fearing that their own 'bad behaviour' has been responsible for what has happened. Added to this is the widespread misconception that most children are in care because they have done something 'wrong'. Worse still, they themselves come to believe that they are blameworthy, perhaps because this common misunderstanding confirms their own fears and sense of guilt.

Much greater community understanding is essential if this is to change.

To bring it about a systematic educational campaign would have to be mounted which incidentally may also increase the pool of people willing to undertake fostering.

9   Granting basic rights to children in care

These include the right to know their own family background; to acquire a sense of continuity in their lives by means of photographs, letters, diaries and the like; to be involved in decisions affecting their future; to be prepared for leaving care and living independently; and the right to privacy. These and many others have been fully spelt out by young people living in care (Page and Clark, 1977).

10   Research needs

The paucity of research, documented in the Bureau's first literature review (Dinnage and Pringle, 1967), has remained virtually unchanged during the past decade. So much so, that the major conclusions reached then, were reprinted in the subsequent review covering the intervening years (Prosser, 1978). Four areas in particular remain in urgent need of further research. All are concerned more with qualitative than quantitative aspects of foster care, although the latter are also inadequately served by available knowledge.

The first relates to exploring the views and feelings of children and young people who have experienced foster care, as well as how they fared as young adults compared with those who have grown up in residential settings. Secondly, qualitative studies of successful placements may improve the selection and preparation of future foster parents; so would a greater understanding of the role of foster fathers and of the family's own children.

The third area is how particularly vulnerable groups have fared in foster homes, for example, ethnic minorities, bereaved children, those who have been abused or the handicapped. Lastly the placement process itself requires systematic monitoring as it takes place: the factors which affect decision-making; the time spent on arranging placements and whether this influences the eventual outcome; the appropriateness of decisions in relation to alternative types of care; the factors which turn short stays into long ones and so on.

Next Steps

We already know enough about the basic needs of children in general and of those who are fostered in particular, to change policy and practice now. Giving more consistent and continuous support to foster parents; offering training in child development; increasing allowances to a more realistic

level; launching more imaginative recruiting and selection procedures; mounting more foster schemes for children considered 'difficult', whether because of age, race or handicap — all of these could be expanded now, given the will and a small shift in resources from residential to foster care. Then in a decade's time, when the Bureau brings out another updating of its foster care review, it will be possible to record improvements in both knowledge and practice.

References

BOWEN, M. (1969) 'Foster care', *Mental Health*, Autumn, pp. 31–3.

COOPER, J.D. (1978) *Patterns of Family Placement: Current Issues in Fostering and Adoption*, National Children's Bureau.

DINNAGE, R. and PRINGLE, M.K. (1967) *Foster Home Care — Facts and Fallacies*, Longman in association with National Children's Bureau.

PAGE, R. and CLARK, G.A. (1977) *Who Cares? Young People in Care Speak Out*, National Children's Bureau.

PARKER, R.A. (1966) *Decision in Child Care: A Study of Prediction in Fostering*, Allen and Unwin.

PRINGLE, M.K. (1971) *Deprivation and Education*, 2nd ed., Longman.

PRINGLE, M.K. (1975) *The Needs of Children*, Hutchinson.

PROSSER, H. (1978) *Perspectives on Foster Care: An Annotated Bibliography*, NFER, for National Children's Bureau.

Chapter 11

The Needs of Handicapped Children and Their Families*

Introduction

The basic assumption underlying what I shall say is that the focus should be on the child and his family in their community and on his developmental needs as a child rather than primarily on a handicapping condition. The physical, emotional, educational and social aspects of the child with special needs must be kept in constant balance with each other. The majority of such children grow up, and will continue to live, in a local community amongst ordinary people. They should be saved as far as possible from isolation and helped towards independence.

The wide range of handicapping conditions, physical, mental, emotional and social — some slight, some severe, some temporary, some permanent — means that it is more appropriate to plan in the light of a child's all-round needs and functional capacities in everyday life, rather than with a too exclusive emphasis on the nature of the defect. But due attention must be given to the important direct and indirect effects on the child of the handicapping condition and the need for treatment and remedial action.

In this interdisciplinary, comprehensive approach, the personal, family and social needs of handicapped children should be given equal weight with those of health and education. All three must play an equal part, though with different roles at different times, in assessing and meeting the needs of handicapped children.

*This paper was originally published in PALMER, J.W. (Ed.) *Special Education in the New Community Services: Report of the 31st National Biennial Conference of the Association for Special Education*, Ron Jones Publications, 1973.

Learning and Emotion

The assumption that emotion and learning are separate and distinct from each other is still widespread. In fact intellect and feelings are so closely interwoven as to be almost indivisible. Furthermore, the basic emotional and educational needs are shared by all children but the presence of a disability poses some special problems. For most practical purposes a four-fold classification is sufficient, namely the need for love and security, for new experiences, for recognition and achievement and for responsibility.

The first need is perhaps the most important during the long and difficult business of growing up. It is unconditional acceptance which gives the child this sense of security of 'belonging', the sense of being cherished whatever he may be like and whatever he may do. This is the basic and all pervasive feature of parental love and of a secure environment — valuing the child for his own sake.

What are the special problems faced by the handicapped in relation to this need? To give a sense of security, one needs to feel secure oneself. But this is just what many parents of a handicapped child do not feel. Some are overwhelmed by their lack of knowledge and afraid that they may not be able to meet his special needs; others feel guilty or ashamed. Some may be completely at a loss to understand the child's difficulties, especially parents of slow-learning children, even if they are themselves of good intelligence, while parents of limited ability are likely to be too bewildered by all the other demands of modern life to give adequate emotional support to their handicapped child.

In the great majority of cases, not enough is done to help the parents of a handicapped child to face and come to terms with their own unconscious attitudes and fears (Tizard and Grad, 1961). At school too, special difficulties are likely to arise unless the child is among the lucky few, for whom an early and correct diagnosis is made, a place is available in a suitable school, whether ordinary or special, and long-term educational guidance, in the fullest sense of the term, as well as social and home support are provided throughout his school life.

It is entirely natural that parents feel concerned and often anxious. Indeed, these feelings could be harnessed to provide the motivation for giving that extra care, time and thought to the handicapped child which are so essential in helping him to overcome as far as possible the adverse effects of a disability.

Instead, this natural concern often turns into over-anxiety or resentment; left without a full understanding of the nature of the handicap or of its short, as well as long-term implications, parental uncertainty may show itself in insecure and inconsistent handling. The more severe, complex or multiple the handicap, the more urgent the need for comprehensive diagnosis and continuous guidance.

The second basic emotional need is for new experiences. For the small baby everything that goes on around him falls into this category; so is every one of his earliest achievements, be it the ability to walk or to examine the texture, taste and appearance of materials and objects; while learning to understand speech and to talk himself, makes possible a vast range of new experiences. New experiences can, in fact, be regarded as a prerequisite for development. A child's ability to learn, to respond to 'socialization' and education in the widest sense of the term, depends not only on inborn capacity or intelligence, but also on the stimulation and opportunity for new experiences provided by his environment.

How does the handicapped child fare regarding the satisfaction of this need? Inevitably the nature of the handicap will delay, or in some cases even make impossible the acquisition of at least some new experiences. Little is known as yet about how each handicap distorts learning; for example the physically handicapped may fail to acquire experience of space and movement which may distort concepts of distance, dimension and later of number; and the deaf, because they remain unstimulated by speech and language until much later, and even then to a more limited extent than normal children, may fail to acquire an adequate basis for abstract thought.

Not only is it inevitable that the early learning of the handicapped child will be affected, but this is a cumulative and progressive process. The precise ways in which it influences the quality of learning await detailed exploration. Meanwhile the ingenuity of parents and teachers will be taxed to the full if they try to provide and adapt new experiences to the child's limitations without curtailing the range of those experiences more than is absolutely necessary.

One effective way of learning, open to all handicapped children except the deaf, is through speech. For some, such as the physically severely disabled, it can be a compensatory way of broadening their experience and understanding. Language and speech play a crucial part in the learning of all children; but talking to the handicapped child and encouraging him to speak from the earliest age is particularly important.

The third need, for recognition and achievement, is closely linked with the previous one. Just because learning may be a slower and more arduous process than for the normal child, a strong incentive is needed. This lies in the pleasure shown at success and in the praise given to achievement by the adults whom the child loves or admires, and wants to please. Encouragement and a reasonable level of expectation act as a spur; too little expectation leads the child to accept too low a standard of effort; too high expectations make him feel that he cannot live up to what is required of him, which leads to discouragement and diminished effort. An optimum level is geared to each child's capability at a given point in time and at a given stage of growth; a level where success is possible, but not without real effort.

In relation to the handicapped child there are twin difficulties here, based on assumptions which are rarely made explicit and of which we are barely conscious. The first is that we habitually praise for achievement, rather than for effort. This is unjust at best and positively harmful at worst. For example, a physically handicapped child may have written only a few lines of composition, but it will have cost him a great deal more in terms of concentration and effort than the bright child needed to produce twice as much; yet the latter is much more likely to be commended for his work. Linked to this is the general tendency to judge the success of the handicapped by the extent to which their achievements equal those of the normal majority. In consequence, the more severe the handicap, the less likely that the child will be rewarded genuinely and unreservedly by recognition and a sense of real achievement.

Thus, if this need is to be met, the handicapped must be granted the fulfilment of another need, aptly described by Mallinson (1956) as 'the need to be different and the need to be the same.' To do so it must not only be recognized that the basic needs are shared by all children but also to make all necessary allowances for the differences imposed upon the handicapped child by the nature of his disability. This means that even the slightest improvement over his previous performance is worthy of praise and recognition; the physically handicapped child who manages to walk a few steps unaided; the deaf child who repeats, though imperfectly, a word previously quite beyond him; in each case the effort deserves recognition. The effort involved in making these small steps forward is colossal compared with the progress made by the normal child with relative ease.

The fourth need, for responsibility, is met by allowing the child to gain personal independence; first through learning to look after himself in feeding, dressing and washing himself; later in permitting him increasing freedom of movement without supervision about the home, street and neighbourhood as well as increasing responsibility for his own possessions; and finally by encouraging him to become entirely self-supporting until eventually he may assume responsibility for others, at work or within his own family.

Inevitably the nature of a child's handicap may set a limit to the ultimate degree of responsibility he will become capable of exercising. But there is a tendency to set too low a limit from a sense of pity or over-protection, or else through underestimating what he might become able to do. Also there is a need to guard against a whole household revolving around the handicapped child; rather he should be given the opportunity both at home and in school to shoulder some responsibilities, however limited in scope, so that he learns to give as well as to receive. In this way, self-respect and self acceptance are fostered. How a child feels about himself and his handicap is a much more potent factor in determining his personal and social adjustment than the nature or even the degree of his disability (Carlson, 1952; Mallinson, 1956; Pringle, 1964).

Supporting the Family

Every parent wants to have a normal child and many mothers fear they may give birth to a deformed one. When this fear becomes a reality, a sense of guilt, feelings of rejection and a determination to make up, almost to atone, to the child for what has happened to him, are all present in various degrees. In most cases, rejection is modified but it may then turn into over-protectiveness and over-possessiveness, which eventually can become as damaging as the disability itself. In addition, there is likely to be some conflict between meeting the needs of the handicapped child on the one hand and those of all the other members of the family on the other hand. And where continuous care is required because of the severity of the handicap, frustration and resentment are inevitable concomitants of coping with such heavy demands.

There is no easy way of helping parents to face and manage their problems, no golden rule and no short cut. However, there is no doubt that the sooner the child's handicap and all its implications are considered as openly but also as supportively as possible, the better for all concerned. As Kershaw (1961) succinctly puts it: 'The temptation to procrastinate may be considerable . . . it is not always necessary to tell the whole truth at once with uncurbed frankness. A spade is a spade; there is no need to call it a "bloody shovel" but it is dishonest and useless to pretend that it is a silver spoon.'

Early, comprehensive, multi-professional and continuous assessment and guidance are essential for every child, and counselling services, both on an individual and a group basis, should be readily available to parents.

Schooling for the Handicapped Child

Because trained intelligence can make up or at least compensate for physical and sensory disabilities, it is essential to consider the child's educational potential early and to plan well ahead for his special needs. Every handicapped child should be looked at periodically as a growing individual whose special problems deserve special attention 'in the round'. This means a physical, psychological and social investigation so that all the factors, which have a bearing on deciding the most suitable educational placement, can be taken into consideration.

The present climate of opinion favours parental and community care. From this it follows that removing a child from his home is considered advisable only if remaining with his family is likely to hinder or even harm his physical, emotional or intellectual development; and that attendance at a special school is advisable only when the ordinary school cannot provide the special methods or equivalent which are needed to ensure the child's progress.

Practice is, of course, far less straightforward, clearcut and tidy. Home and community care can only work if the community cares in the sense of providing the necessary supportive and ancillary services. These range from adaptation of houses and classrooms, to home helps, counselling part-time specialist teachers and special day schools within manageable travelling distance.

Some ideas, such as a comprehensive school for the various types of handicaps, have hardly been tried out in this country except for the severely multi-handicapped child; also practices such as weekly boarding, and fostering with families in the neighbourhood for children who have to attend residential schools far from their homes, could be adopted on a much wider scale than hitherto. By such means the need for 'parentectomy' would be eliminated or at least substantially reduced.

Recognition of the importance of early learning has clear educational implications for handicapped children. Preschool provision is as vital. The ideal is nursery schools and classes willing and able to accept a few handicapped children; play groups also have a contribution to make, provided guidance from trained, experienced advisers is available.

Acceptance of the 1944 Education Act dictum that education should take account of a child's 'age, ability and aptitude' has as its corollary the need for variety, flexibility and continuity of provision. This is even more essential for the handicapped than for ordinary pupils. Continuity is perhaps most important of all; partly because early learning is likely to have been delayed and partly because subsequent progress may be at a slower than normal pace on account of the handicapping condition. As a result many children will not be ready — scholastically or emotionally — to leave the world of school and further training at sixteen or even seventeen years.

If the opportunity for remaining in either a full-time or part-time educational setting were to be continued as late as twenty-five years of age, many more might well become able to earn their living, or at least to make a substantial contribution to it. This applies particularly to educationally subnormal youngsters. For many handicapped adolescents a halfway house of work experience combined with continued schooling would not only cushion the transition from school to work but might well turn out to be a financial investment in terms of reduced unemployment among the handicapped.

Education in How to Live with a Handicap

To be handicapped is to belong to a minority group. This always poses some problems of relationships; being unable to do and live like the majority creates a sense of isolation; consciousness of being different makes the handicapped person awkward or shy which calls out similar reactions in the normal. Moreover, few of the non-handicapped majority are completely at ease in the company of the handicapped.

Attitudes towards physical disabilities vary widely, covering the whole range of emotions from sympathy to ridicule; the limbless are pitied while the stammerer or clubfoot are mimicked. Visibility (i.e. how obvious) and appearance (i.e. how ugly or malformed) also determine the degree of acceptance or tolerance.

Towards children these general attitudes are usually modified by a protective pity. While this shields them during their most vulnerable years, at the same time it must make their entry into the adult world a baffling and painful, if not traumatic, experience. A sympathetic, compassionate and almost overprotective world inexplicably turns into one of embarrassed, evasive, irritated people.

Education in how to live with a handicap must have its roots in a deliberate and realistic appraisal of the possible. In the first place this has to be made for the young child jointly by all those concerned for his care, management and education. It begins in the home and for many years to come parents will provide this education.

Meeting the child's basic emotional needs in appropriate ways is one part of this education; gradually teaching the child a clear-sighted acceptance of possibilities (and inevitable limitations) is another; helping him through periods of resentment, bitterness, apathy and despair is perhaps the most difficult and painful part when parental hopes and ambitions have also been sadly disappointed. A consoling, healing and encouraging experience for parent and child can be to meet similarly handicapped children and adults, both those struggling like themselves and those who have successfully faced, or better still triumphed over, equal or worse obstacles. Knowing what can be achieved helps to maintain high but realistic standards as well as high morale.

It is not only the disabled child who has to learn how to live with his handicap. Each member of his family must find a way of doing so. That the father's support is quite crucial has been clearly shown in previous studies. Where he is able and willing to share the responsibilities and anxieties of caring for the handicapped child, there is a much greater chance of the marriage and family life itself remaining unimpaired or even being enhanced through sharing a labour of love.

Education for recreation comes a close second to education for employment. Hobbies, the various arts, games such as chess or cards, and also certain physical sports may well be within the child's capacity; indeed, some, like swimming and riding, can be of therapeutic value. Not only do recreational pursuits provide bridges to the world of the non-handicapped, they also provide opportunities to make relations with the opposite sex during adolescence, when most young people are looking for romance and eventually marriage. This is a particularly neglected aspect of education in living with a handicap, probably because it is so fraught with hurt, damaged self-esteem and, most important of all, because there are no easy or ready answers.

Thus it becomes apparent that education in how to live with a handicap must be much wider than merely help for the child concerned. It must include attention to the likely effects on parents, siblings and neighbours; indeed it is the community which needs to be helped towards greater understanding so that it wills the means necessary to improve the quality of life and of the opportunities open to the handicapped child and his family.

All this, every handicapped young person must face sooner or later; if he can do so with the help of a compassionate, understanding and honest adult, then his (and, even more so, her) learning will be that much less difficult. Getting to know handicapped people who have made successful marriages may give hope. For some, marriage will be an unlikely goal. The knowledge that some people are successfully and happily wedded to their work or hobby, and through these make firm friendships, may be a consolation if not an aim.

References

CARLSON, E.R. (1952) *Born That Way*, Arthur James, The Drift, Evesham.
KERSHAW, J.D. (1961) *Handicapped Children*, Heinemann.
MALLINSON, V. (1956) *None Can Be Called Deformed*, Heinemann.
PRINGLE, M.K. (1970) *The Challenge of Thalidomide*, Longman.
PRINGLE, M.K. (1964, reprinted 1969) *The Emotional and Social Adjustment of Physically Handicapped Children*, Occ. Public No. II National Foundation for Educational Research, Slough, Bucks.

TANSLEY, A.E. and GULLIFORD, R. (1960) *The Education of Slow Learning Children*, Routledge and Kegan Paul.

TIZARD, J. and GRAD, J.C. (1961) *The Mentally Handicapped and their Families*, Oxford University Press.

YOUNGHUSBAND, E., BIRCHALL, D., DAVIE, R. and PRINGLE, M.K. (Eds) (1970) *Living with Handicap*, National Children's Bureau.

Chapter 12

Towards the Prediction of Child Abuse*

How many children in this country are seriously ill-treated by their parents (or permanent substitutes), physically, psychologically or both? How many are permanently maimed or killed as a consequence of such abuse? That the answers to these questions are not at present known with any degree of certainty is itself quite significant because to a considerable extent it reflects common attitudes to this problem. They are a mixture of revulsion, disbelief and plain ignorance. There is repugnance or sheer disbelief, not only among the general public but some professional workers too, that a parent could kill his or her own child; for example, 'many courts in the United Kingdom have only just begun to believe that child abuse truly exists' (Kempe and Kempe, 1978). Ignorance extends even to doctors, who are either unaware of the syndrome or avoid confrontation by ascribing death to an associated existing clinical entity (Howells, 1975).

Another reason why the extent of the problem is not known is because parents (and others) do not always kill their children in easily ascertainable ways which can be identified by pathologists and classified into accidental and non-accidental categories. Thus some of the causes of death given in the Registrar General's statistics for England and Wales may not be as innocent as the designation implies. Examples are deaths from pneumonia or bronchitis in infants who have failed to thrive because of physical or emotional neglect; poisonings (Rogers *et al.* 1976); suffocation caused by pressing a hand or pillow against a baby's face; deaths following intra-cerebral and subdural haemorrhages after shaking; and deaths from a multiplicity of causes among severely subnormal children whose handicap itself originated from a battering months or years previously (Oliver, 1975; Buchanan and Oliver, 1977).

There are two common misconceptions. One is that we are all

*This chapter originally appeared as Chapter 14 in FRUDE, N. (Ed.) (1980) *Psychological Approaches to Child Abuse*, Batsford Academic and Educational.

potential batterers and that the main causes are depression and poverty. In fact, most parents who violently assault their children are young, immature, ill-educated, disorganized and aggressive; many of the fathers involved have criminal records. Their incomes are similar to those of non-battering families, but they organize their finances badly (Smith, 1975).

The other misconception is that child abuse is very rare. In fact, at a conservative estimate some 8000 children suffer 'non-accidental injuries' every year and about 110 babies are battered to death; in addition, every day one infant under a year old is brain-damaged as a result of parental violence, some becoming blind or paralyzed for the rest of their lives. Moreover, all those who have made a special study of the problem are now agreed that these are only the tip of an iceberg since reported cases represent only a fraction of the total (Cooper, 1978; Kempe and Kempe, 1978). Thousands more grow up maladjusted and severely disturbed because they have been emotionally neglected, rejected and abused.

Psychological Consequence of Abuse

Remarkably little attention has so far been paid to the likely psychological consequences of child abuse compared with the considerable and still expanding literature on the problems and needs of their parents. The same discrepancy is evident between the emphasis on supporting and treating the violent and abusing adult on the one hand and, on the other hand, the almost total lack of support and treatment services for the child victim — except for the physical injuries.

Similarly, there is a great volume of research on the parents' socio-economic background, health, personality, marital and personal history (Jobling, 1976). In contrast, scant attention has been given to the emotional, social and intellectual effects on children of being subjected to parental violence, or of growing up rejected and ill-treated, even though not to the point of maiming or death. This apparent lack of concern for the psycho-logical consequences is mirrored too in all the official reports of Committees of Inquiry into fatal cases, starting with Maria Colwell in 1974 right to the present day. None of them even refer to likely emotional damage arising from physical abuse. Yet this must surely have been evident in most cases long before the final tragedy? (DHSS, 1974; DHSS, 1975a; 1975b; Lambeth *et al.* 1975; Norfolk, 1976.)

It was undoubtedly so in the case of six-year-old Maria Colwell. Within a period of fifteen months she changed from being a happy, responsive, well-behaved, attractive little girl, who was making good progress at school and getting on well with other children, to becoming withdrawn, solitary, depressed, unable to communicate, sitting for hours staring into space, and not responding to children or adults. She began wetting and soiling her bed, shunned other children and her school work deteriorated markedly. Indeed, the descriptions of her behaviour shortly before she was killed by her stepfather indicated clearly that she was in a state of severe shock, depression and deep mourning for the 'parents' she had lost — namely, the foster parents with whom she had lived practically all her life.

But it was not only that her appearance and behaviour deteriorated rapidly after she was made to leave her foster home. When in preparation for the move she was taken to spend days and then weekends in her mother's home, Maria clearly showed her dislike and fear of these visits by the most strenuous protests, both verbally and physically. She began to show stress symptoms, such as biting her nails, being unable to go to sleep and was, in fact, prescribed a 'nerve tonic' by her doctor. When made to stay overnight at her mother's home, she ran away half-dressed and barefoot on several occasions.

Thus from the outset, Maria displayed unmistakable signs of great psychological strain and unhappiness — signs which required hardly any psychological or psychiatric skill to interpret. And a minimal knowledge of normal child development is sufficient to appreciate that running away in the middle of the night is a sign of real desperation and terror in a six-year-old.

The treatment subsequently meted out to her by both her mother and stepfather — exploitation, under-nourishment, imprisonment and violence — destroyed her not only physically but emotionally too. Yet apparently none of those professionally concerned — teachers, social workers, health visitors and doctors — considered her to be in need of psychological support or treatment, and even during the enquiry into her death no reference was made to the psychological warning signs which should have been heeded as much as the physical symptoms of her suffering (DHSS, 1974).

Among abused infants, behavioural indicators may not be as dramatic or clear cut as physical injury, and hence are more difficult to explore. Nevertheless, experienced paediatricians and psychologists can determine whether developmental progress is normal or gives cause for concern, calling for closer enquiry. Unless there is a recognized, diagnosed physical cause, all 'non-thriving' children should be given a comprehensive psycho-social assessment which should include an elucidation of how the child himself sees his family. It is possible to obtain this picture at a very much younger age than is sometimes realized, even by some professionals. In addition to systematically observing the infant's behaviour, play and capacity for making relationships with friendly adults, a range of more structured instruments for assessing personality is available (Bene and Anthony, 1957; Geddis *et al.*, 1977; Howells and Lickorish, 1962; Jackson, 1952; Pickford, 1963).

It remains a matter for conjecture and disquiet why the importance and relevance of the psychological consequences of abuse should have remained a largely ignored issue, not only as early warning signals but also later on as criteria indicating whether or not a child should be returned to its previously abusing home. Similarly overlooked have been the likely psychological effects on the siblings of observing and living with the daily reality of a brother or sister being neglected, rejected or abused, whether physically, emotionally, or both. One would suspect these to be deeply disturbing and hence at least as deserving of treatment as the adult perpetrators.

Another largely unexplored area is that of the long-term consequences of child abuse. The few available follow-up studies indicate severe and lasting disturbance and malfunctioning, even when there is no further physical ill-treatment (Oliver and Cox, 1973; Martin and Beezley, 1977; Strauss and Girodet, 1977; Jones, 1978). Hence even from the point of view of cost effectiveness — let alone the equally if not more important humane considerations — it is vital to work towards developing more adequate methods of prediction and prevention.

The Possibility of Prediction

Prediction will require complex, multi-dimensional and in-depth methods since abusing parents are unlikely to be a homogeneous group, either regarding their personalities or their social background; nor is there likely to be one set of common causal factors or predisposing conditions which bring about their behaviour. Failure to differentiate between all these may well account for the rather confused body of research findings. There are at least four different approaches to prediction which are not mutually exclusive: the first is to distinguish, as far as present knowledge permits, between the different motives of parents who violently assault their children; the second is to consider the likely long-term psychological effects of abuse on children which in turn will make them more liable as adults to become abusing parents themselves; the third approach is to explore how early it is possible to detect danger signals that a baby's future safety and well-being may be 'at risk'; and the fourth is to examine the availability of checklists systematizing the insight and knowledge obtained from the first three approaches.

Patterns of Parental Violence

As I see it, there are several sets of circumstances which may lead to a child being seriously abused. There is the isolated incident which is unlikely to be repeated. In this category is the mother or father who has no previous history of violence, who has coped adequately with the stresses and strains of everyday life, and who may have brought up other children quite well. Then some disaster strikes or there is an accumulation of stressful events which lead to a sudden outburst of anger in which a hitherto well-cared for and loved child is injured, followed by shame and remorse. Such a violent incident could not have been predicted, nor is its recurrence likely since it is quite out of character.

Another pattern represents a persisting and potentially dangerous parental attitude, namely where one child is singled out for ill-treatment. Reasons for such 'scapegoating' include the child who is a pre-marital or extra-marital 'mistake', or who reminds the mother of a despised husband or a hated relative, or the child who is felt to be in some way 'different' from the other children. This difference may be due to a difficult delivery or to pre-maturity or to early 'bonding failure'; or the baby may have some physical or mental handicap with which the parent cannot come to terms. The rejection and ill-treatment in such cases are child-specific, and hence none of the siblings are at a similar risk. Recurrence is likely unless the mother is able and willing to work through her hostility with psychiatric help. If instead she chooses to relinquish the child, she should be supported through this course of action.

Probably a more numerous group liable to neglect and ill-treat their children are inadequate parents. They include teenage couples who additionally may be immature even for their ages; those of limited abilities who themselves have often been neglected, if not ill-treated, in childhood; and those who have grown up in institutional care. Such parents often lack knowledge of normal child development. For example, they do not understand that a baby is unable to stop soiling or wetting until he has reached the necessary stage of physical maturity, or that a terrified infant may fail to acquire sphincter and bowel control just because he is terrified.

Environmental pressures, such as inadequate housing, poverty, and too many or too closely spaced pregnancies, may further add to the parents' inability to cope. Often too the child has been neither planned nor wanted and, even more crucial, may remain unwanted. All these features are chronic and so neither quick nor profound change can realistically be expected. Therefore the children inevitably remain at risk unless frequent, continuous and long-term support services can be given, including intensive training in homemaking and child-rearing skills. The outlook even then is not always hopeful.

Violence as a way of life characterizes a a group of parents who can be predicted to constitute the greatest risk to their children's safety. Their habitually violent behaviour is directed not only towards their offspring but also towards each other, as well as their neighbours, relatives and work-mates. Among them are found the psychopath who lashes out indiscriminately; the mentally ill, including the delusional schizophrenic; the pathologically authoritarian parent, more often male, who continually punishes a child for failing to come up to his unrealistically high demands; and the sadistic pervert who gains satisfaction from the suffering of the weak and helpless.

Probably most, if not all such parents, were themselves damaged in childhood through an uncaring or violent upbringing. So parental hostility perpetuates itself from one generation to another in what is quite literally a very vicious circle. Thus, to allow a child to remain or return to such a home perpetuates the pattern of violence in the long term. In the short term it puts even the child's physical welfare at risk. There is no reliable way to ensure his safety since there is no known effective and quick enough treatment which will modify the behaviour of adults for whom violence is a way of life.

Predicting the Long-term Effects of Abuse as Being Self-perpetuating

Since there is as yet inadequate research evidence, I shall consider the likely effects of child abuse on long-term development in the light of what is known about the needs of children (Pringle, 1975 and 1978). To begin with, an abused child's sense of security and of being valued is bound to become undermined, if indeed it has ever been established. When rejection and ill-treatment are intermittent, then he or she lives in a state of constant uncertainty, never knowing what to expect; these may be the children whose attitude has been described as one of 'frozen watchfulness'. When abuse is continuous, then either submission or anger will become the typical reaction.

The child who submits is likely to develop a 'victim' mentality, attempting to appease, to ingratiate himself, even clinging to the abusing parent; or he may withdraw, trying to become inconspicuous, but remaining chronically apprehensive. On the other hand, the child who responds with anger and defiance is liable to provoke a battle of wills, making the abusing adult determined 'to show who is master'. Since a child cannot be 'made' to do anything — be it to keep down food, stop crying or go to sleep — and since the immature, violent parent finds his own impotence unacceptable, a headlong clash is as inevitable as its tragic outcome.

The ill-treated baby is in an even more desperate plight than the young child because he is as yet physically incapable of responding to force and pain in one or other of the natural ways, namely, either fight or flight: he can no more hit back than run away. Hence, ill-treatment may well arouse helpless rage and hate, which will then be carried into adult life to become the smouldering anger of the wife or child batterer (Pizzey, 1974); or the equivalent of Harlow's (1969) female monkeys, 'hopeless, helpless and heartless mothers' who either ignore or brutally abuse their offspring.

A preliminary study of wife battering concludes that 'fear must be expressed for the 315 children of the 100 women reported, as many males are developing the prodromal signs of violence while the older age groups manifest a disturbing picture of uncontrolled violence and conflict with the law. Unless an urgent retraining programme can be undertaken with these children a future generation will be subjected to family violence' (Gayford, 1975). This vicious circle of intergenerational neglect and violence has been confirmed by other evidence, which also shows that children from violent families not only tend to marry early but to have large families (Martin, 1976; Frommer and O'Shea, 1973b; Rutter and Madge, 1976).Then they in turn fail to provide love and security for their offspring, having been unloved and rejected in their own childhood.

Next, when the need for new experiences remains inadequately met, then intellectual potentialities as well as personal growth remain to some extent unrealized. In the infant, insufficient sensory stimulation can retard or even impair development, including later on the ability to think, reason and communicate. Since the great majority of neglected and ill-treated children come from socially and culturally deprived families, they would in any case be adversely affected by the relative lack of stimulation in such homes. However, their plight is likely to be worse. To begin with, the abused baby has to spend much of his time lying in his cot, lonely, uncomfortable and probably in pain; such conditions stifle exploration and curiosity and hence 'learning'.

Next, while trying to cope with new demands — such as to feed less messily, or to become dry and clean — he is bound to be slow and to make 'mistakes' just because he is immature and a beginner. He will then be meted out punishment for what is seen by the inadequate or violent parent as defiance or lack of love. The resulting anxiety and fear will inevitably retard or inhibit adequate learning. And so the infant is caught in an unending spiral of unrealistic demands, failure to improve and consequent punishment.

If brain damage results, then, of course, improvement becomes even less possible, the more so the more severe the impairment. Once he becomes a mobile toddler, who naturally wants to explore his surroundings, his 'being into everything' is also likely to arouse parental anger, as will his normal attempts to assert his own will. Thus his striving towards knowledge and independence will be stifled through fear and punishment. Hence it is not unexpected that follow-up studies of abused children report their development to be retarded, both in the neuro-motor and intellectual fields, as well as in the acquisition of language skills (Martin and Beezley, 1977; Strauss and Girodet, 1977).

Turning now to the need for praise and recognition, when this is inadequately met, then in the long term the effects are destructive of self-respect and of confidence in tackling new situations, tasks and relationships. There can be little doubt that the abused child will be among the most serious under-achievers since — almost by definition — he is under-valued and rejected. Even ability and talent well above average may never declare themselves if adequate nurture and emotional support are lacking (Pringle, 1970). Rather than calling out compassion, his backwardness and under-functioning themselves compound his plight by apparently justifying parental punishment. Thus their rejection carries the seeds of his continued failure to come up to their expectations and so it becomes inexorably a self-fulfilling prophecy.

Lastly, with regard to the need for responsibility, the abused child is likely all too often to suffer simultaneously from being given both too little and too much responsibility. On the one hand, he may be deprived of toys over which he can excercise exclusive rights; he may be denied sufficient practice to learn to feed and dress himself because he is considered to be too slow and clumsy; and he may also lack opportunities of acquiring the responsibility of give-and-take in the company of other children. On the other hand, he may far too early be left to fend for himself; also he, or perhaps more often she, may be made into a household drudge. In any case, the child will all too often be punished for what is seen as unhelpful or irresponsible behaviour. Yet he has little chance to improve upon past performance because of being denied the relaxed and unhurried practice of those very skills which would enable him in time to act responsibly. So the basis is laid for later avoidance of responsibility.

In summary, a consideration of the likely long-term psychological effects of abuse strongly suggests that it will to a greater or lesser extent impair emotional, social and intellectual development because a violent upbringing makes it impossible to meet a child's basic psychological needs. Hence, as an adult, he or she will be more liable to become an inadequate and probably abusing parent in turn.

How Early is Prediction Possible?

Recent evidence suggests that prediction is possible before or soon after a baby's birth (Frommer and O'Shea, 1973a and 1973b; Lynch and Roberts, 1977; Wolkind, 1977; Cooper, 1978; Kempe and Kempe, 1978). Several screening procedures have been developed which take into account such factors as the parents' own childhood experiences, their marital relationship, feelings about the pregnancy and expectations about their unborn child. For example, a series of danger signals has been identified in the delivery room, the most significant of which seemed to be a mother responding passively to her baby (i.e. not touching, holding or examining it); either parent reacting to it with hostility; neither of them looking into the baby's eyes; and not being affectionate towards each other. The observations made in the labour wards and delivery rooms were found to make over 76 per cent correct predictions regarding successful or unsuccessful parenting (Kempe and Kempe, 1978).

Another series of studies has been concerned with the development of the reciprocal relationship between mother and baby immediately after its birth and with the factors which promote mother-infant bonding (Ainsworth *et al.*, 1974; Brazelton *et al.*, 1974; Ringler *et al.*, 1975; Klaus and Kennel, 1976; de Chateau and Wiberg, 1977 and 1978). These too provide persuasive evidence of the diagnostic importance of observing the earliest interactions between adult and child.

Checklists of Characteristics Common to Abusing Parents and to Abused Children

A wide range of early warning signals that a child may be at high risk of being abused is now available. However, there is no agreed range of predictors and the number suggested varies from study to study (from half a dozen to over seventy). Preparing and using checklists, as well as keeping 'at risk' registers, are useful aids for professional workers in alerting them to those features which tend to characterize abusing parents and abused children. None can be regarded, however, as a substitute for a comprehensive and detailed assessment of each family and for an equally comprehensive developmental examination of each child.

Below some examples are given of checklists which set out a series of characteristics common to abusive parents and abused children.

I *Characteristics Common to Abusive Parents* (Steele, 1975)
  1 Immature and dependent
  2 Social isolation
  3 Poor self-esteem
  4 Difficulty seeking or obtaining pleasure
  5 Distorted perceptions of the child, and often role-reversal
  6 Fear of spoiling the child
  7 Belief in the value of punishment
  8 Impaired ability to empathize with the child's needs and respond appropriately

II *Factors Clearly Differentiating an Abused Group from a Control Group* (Lynch and Roberts, 1978)
  1 More abusing mothers were under twenty years when they had their first children: 50 per cent compared with 16 per cent.
  2 Abusing mothers were more likely to have signs of emotional disturbance recorded in the maternity notes: 46 per cent compared with 14 per cent.
  3 More abusing parents were referred to the maternity hospital social worker; 58 per cent compared with 6 per cent.
  4 The abused babies were more likely to have been admitted to the special care baby nursery: 42 per cent compared with 10 per cent.
  5 The abusing mothers more often evoked concern over their mothering capacity: 44 per cent compared with 6 per cent.

III *Key Characteristics of Child Abuse* (Hanson, McCulloch and Hartley, 1978)
  1 *Parental characteristics*
    Mother under twenty years old at birth of first child
    Mother has psychiatric diagnosis of neuroticism
    Mother has high neuroticism score on Eysenck Personality Inventory
    Mother has psychiatric diagnosis of personality disorder
    Father has psychiatric diagnosis of personality disorder
    Mother has borderline or subnormal intelligence on a short form of the Wechsler Adult Intelligence Scale
    Father has a manual occupation
    Mother has a criminal record
    Father has a criminal record
    Mother has a high General Health Questionnaire score

Mother has an abnormal EEG
Father has an abnormal EEG

2 *Social characteristics of the families*
Child's natural father absent from the home
Mother unmarried
Parents acquainted less than six months before marriage
Mother conceived premaritally
Mother considers the marriage unsatisfactory
Battered child illegitimate
Mother thinks her partner rejects the child
Mother says there is no discussion about child-rearing
Mother considers herself the decision-maker in the house
Child lacks his own room
Accommodation lacks one or more basic amenities
Mother rarely sees her parents
Mother rarely sees any relatives
Mother has no opportunities for breaks from child
Mother has no social activities
Mother has no friends
Mother considers her allowance inadequate
Mother is generally dissatisfied with her situation

3 *Interpersonal relations*
Mother was unhappy in childhood
Mother recalls two or more childhood neurotic symptoms
Mother thinks she was a poor scholar
Mother got on badly with her parents as a child
Mother's mother scolded her as a chief means of punishment
Mother gets on badly with her parents now
Mother had bad relations with siblings as a child
Mother gets on badly with siblings now
Father's mother was unreasonable in discipline
Father's father was unreasonable in discipline
Mother's mother was unreasonable in discipline
Mother's father was unreasonable in discipline
Mother has a high 'lie' score in the Eysenck Personality Inventory
Mother scores high on criticism of others, paranoid hostility and
guilt on the hostility and direction of hostility questionnaire
Father scores high on guilt

4 *Child-rearing practices*
Mother is abnormal (very quick or very slow) in responsiveness to
the child's crying
Mother becomes emotional over feeding problems

Mother is now very demonstrative towards the child
Mother is abnormal in her enjoyment of the child (says she finds no pleasure in him or he is 'her life')
Infrequent surveillance of child's well-being or whereabouts
Obedience expected at second or third request
Mother physically punishes frequently
Father physically punishes frequently
Mother withholds love as a punishment
Mother uses tangible rewards (pacifiers) for good behaviour
Crying in baby or clinging and whining in toddler a problem
Partner does not help mother with child as she would like

5 *The child*

Has a general developmental quotient of 90 or under on the Griffiths Scales of Mental Development
Physically neglected on admission to hospital
Has a history of failure to thrive
Mother says he is not wakeful (half hour plus) at night
Mother says he is not excitable or lively by day
Mother says he is not tired during the day
There is delay in bringing the child to hospital for attention to the injury
Had low birth weight

IV *Factors in the Parents' History which Predict Risk Extremely Accurately* (Kempe and Kempe, 1978)

1 As a child was the parent repeatedly beaten or deprived?
2 Does the parent have a record of mental illness or criminal activities?
3 Is the parent suspected of physical abuse in the past?
4 Is the parent suffering lost self-esteem, social isolation, or depression?
5 Has the parent experienced multiple stresses, such as marital discord, divorce, debt, frequent moves, significant losses?
6 Does the parent have violent outbursts of temper?
7 Does the parent have rigid, unrealistic expectations of the child's behaviour?
8 Does the parent punish the child harshly?
9 Does the parent see the child as difficult and provocative (whether or not the child is)?
10 Does the parent reject the child or have difficulty forming a bond with the child?

V *Untreatable Families where Early Termination of Parental Rights is Indicated* (Kempe and Kempe, 1978)
  1 Cruel abusers who might torture their children slowly and repetitively
  2 Psychotics whose children form part of their delusional systems or borderline psychotic patients not amenable to treatment
  3 Aggressive sociopaths who might unpredictably and lethally strike out when angered
  4 Fanatics, outwardly reasonable, respectable people with an encapsulated psychosis that could kill their children (such as a couple who believed their baby should live only on carrot juice, since all other food was poisonous)
  5 Parents so addicted to alcohol or drugs that they cannot provide even minimal care for their babies
  6 Parents too retarded or mothers simply too young to raise children
  7 Families where other children have already been seriously injured, and where there may have been one or more unexplained deaths

VI *High Risk Rating Check List* (Greenland, 1979)

Parents	*Child*
Previously having abused, neglected a child	Was previously abused or neglected
Age 24 years or less at birth of first child	Under five years of age at the time of abuse or neglect
Single-parent or separated	Premature or low birthweight
Partner not biological parent	Now underweight
History of abuse, neglect or deprivation	Birth defect, chronic illness, developmental lag
Socially isolated, frequent moves, poor housing	Prolonged separation from mother
Poverty, unemployed or unskilled worker	Cries frequently, difficult to comfort
Inadequate education	Difficulties in feeding and elimination
Abuses alcohol and/or drugs	Adopted, foster or step child
History of criminal assaultive behaviour and/or suicide attempts	
Pregnancy, post partum or chronic illesss	

VII *Clinical features in the Abused Child* (Cooper, 1978)
  1 Physical injuries – non-accidental
    Bruises, weals, lacerations and scars
    Burns and scalds
    Bone and joint injuries
    Brain and eye injuries
    Internal injuries
  2 Other clinical disorders
    Poisoning
    Drowning
    Cot deaths
    'Funny turns'
    Repeated problems with crying and feeding
    Overactivity and demanding behaviour
    Hysterical moods (in older children)
  3 Failure to thrive without organic cause
  4 Disordered behaviour (observed)
  5 Sexual abuse
  6 Abuse while in care

VIII *Characteristics Commonly noted in Abused Children in Addition to Developmental Delay* (Martin and Beezley, 1977)
  1 Impaired capacity for enjoyment
  2 Psychiatric symptoms, e.g. enuresis, restlessness and tantrums
  3 Low self esteem
  4 School learning problems
  5 Withdrawal
  6 Rebelliousness
  7 Compulsivity
  8 Hypervigilance
  9 Pseudo-mature behaviour or role reversal

An examination of these various check lists shows a number of recurring features which appear to characterize families in which child abuse is more likely to occur. Ten of these seem to be most common, thus indicating that children in such circumstances are at a potentially greater risk than others. These can be summarized as follows:

  1 One or both parents have, when young themselves, been subjected to violence
  2 One or both parents have had an unhappy, disrupted and insecure childhood
  3 One or both parents are addicted to drugs, alcohol, or are psychotic

4 There is a record of violence between the parents
5 Another child has already been abused, or suffered an unexplained death
6 The pregnancy was unwanted; the baby was rejected at birth or soon after
7 Failure of early bonding
8 Both parents are under twenty years of age, immature for their years and socially isolated
9 The family live in poor housing and on a low income
10 The family is suffering from multiple deprivation

References

AINSWORTH, M.D.S., BELL, S.M. and STAYTON, D.J. (1974) 'Infant-mother attachment and social development: socialization as a product of reciprocal responsiveness to signals', in RICHARDS, M.P.M. (Ed.) *The Integration of a Child into a Social World*, Cambridge University Press.

BAHER, E. *et al.* (1976) *At Risk: An Account of the Work of the Battered Child Research Department of the NSPCC*, Routledge and Kegan Paul.

BENE, E., and ANTHONY, E.J. (1957) *Manual for the Family Relations Test*, Slough, National Foundation for Educational Research.

BRAZELTON, T.B., KOSLOWSKI, B. and MAIN, M. (1974) 'The origins of reciprocity in mother/infant interaction', in LEWIS, M. and ROSENBLUM, A. (Eds.), *The Effect of the Infant on its Caregiver*, John Wiley and Sons.

BUCHANAN, A. and OLIVER, J.E. (1977) 'Abuse and neglect as a cause of mental retardation', *B.J. Psychiatry*, 131, pp. 458–67.

CAMERON, J.M. and RAE, L.J. (1975) *Atlas of the Battered Child Syndrome*, Churchill Livingstone.

COOPER, C. (1978) 'Child abuse and neglect — medical aspects', in SMITH, S.M. (Ed.) *The Maltreatment of Children*, MTP Press Ltd.

DE CHATEAU, P. and WIBERG, B. (1978) 'Long-term effects on mother-infant behaviour of extra contact during the first hour post-partum', in *Psychosomatic Medicine of Obstetrics and Gynaecology*, Basel, S. Karger.

DE CHATEAU, P. and WIBERG, B. (1977) 'Long-term effects on mother-infant behaviour of extra contact during the first hour post-partum. 1. First observation at 36 hours.' *Acta Paediatr.Scand.* 66, p. 137. 2. A follow-up at three months.' *Acta Paediatr.Scand.* 66, p. 145.

Department of Health and Social Security (1975a) *Report of the Committee of Inquiry into the Provision and Coordination of Services to the Family of John George Auckland*, HMSO.

Department of Health and Social Security (1975b) *Non-accidental Injury to Children. Proceedings of a Conference held in June 1974*, HMSO.

Department of Health and Social Security (1974) *Report of the Committee of Inquiry into the Care and Supervision provided in relation to Maria Colwell*, HMSO.

FROMMER, E.A. and O'SHEA, G. (1973a) 'Ante-natal identification of women liable to have problems in managing their infants', *B.J. Psychiatry*, 123, p. 149.

FROMMER, E.A. and O'SHEA, G. (1973b) 'The importance of childhood experience in relation to problems of marriage and family building', *B.J. Psychiatry*, 123, p. 157.

GAYFORD, J.J. (1975) 'Wife battering — a preliminary survey of 100 cases', *B.M.J.* 5951.

GEDDIS, D.C., TURNER, I.F. and EARDLEY, J. (1977) 'Diagnostic value of a psychological test in cases of suspected child abuse', *Archives of Disease in Childhood*, 52, pp. 708–12.

GREENLAND, C. (1979) 'A checklist to recognize a possible situation for child abuse', *Contact*, McMaster Univ. 10, p. 23.

HANSON, R., McCULLOCH, W. and HARTLEY, S. (1978) 'Key characteristics of child abuse', in WHITE FRANKLIN, A. (Ed.), *Child Abuse*, Churchill Livingstone.

HARLOW, H.F. and HARLOW, M.K. (1969) 'Effects of various mother-infant relationships on rhesus monkey behaviour' in FOSS, B. (Ed.) *Determinants of Infant Behaviour*, Methuen.

HOWELLS, J.G. (1975) 'Deaths from non-accidental injuries in childhood', *B.M.J.* 5984, 13 September.

HOWELLS, J.G. and LICKORISH, J.R. (1962) *Manual for the Family Relations Indicator*, National Foundation for Educational Research, Slough.

JACKSON, L. (1952) *A Test of Family Attitudes*, Methuen.

JOBLING, M. (1976) *The Abused Child. An Annotated Bibliography*, National Children's Bureau.

JONES, C. OKELL (1978) 'Meeting the needs of abused children', *Social Work Today*, 9, 26, pp. 9–14.

KEEN, J.H., LANDRUM, J. and WOLMAN, B. (1975) 'Inflicted burns and scalds in children', *B.M.J.* 5991, 1 November.

KEMPE, R.S. and KEMPE, C.H. (1978) *Child Abuse*, Fontana/Open Books Original.

KLAUS, M.H. and KENNEL, J.H. (1976) *Maternal-Infant Bonding*, St Louis, C.V. Mosby.

LAMBETH, SOUTHWARK and LEWISHAM AREA HEALTH AUTHORITY (Teaching); the Inner London Probation and After Care Committee; and the London Borough of Lambeth (1975) *Report of the Joint Committee of Inquiry into Non-Accidental Injury to Children with particular reference to the Case of Lisa Godfrey*, London Borough of Lambeth.

LYNCH, M.A. (1978) 'The prognosis of child abuse', *J. Child Psychol. Psychiat.*, 19, pp. 175–80.

LYNCH, M.A. and ROBERTS, J. (1978) 'Early alerting signs', in WHITE FRANKLIN A. (Ed.) *Child Abuse*, Churchill Livingstone.

LYNCH, M.A. and ROBERTS, J. (1977) 'Prediction of child abuse — signs of bonding failure in the maternity hospital', *B.M.J.*, 1, p. 624.

MARTIN, H.P. (Ed.) (1976) *The Abused Child: A Multi-disciplinary Approach to Development Issues and Treatment*, Ballinger, Cambridge, Mass.

MARTIN, H.P. and BEEZLEY, P. (1977) 'Behavioural observations of abused children', *Devl. Med. Child Neurol.*, 19, pp. 373–87.

NORFOLK COUNTY COUNCIL, and NORFOLK AREA HEALTH AUTHORITY (1976) *Report of the Review Body Appointed to Enquire into the Case of Steven Meurs, 1975*, Norfolk County Council.

OLIVER, J.E. (1975) 'Statistics of child abuse', *B.M.J.*, 5975, 12 July.

OLIVER, J.E. and COX, J. (1973) 'A family kindred with ill-used children', *B.J.Psychiatry*, 123.

PICKFORD, R.W. (1963) *Pickford Projective Pictures*, Tavistock Publications.

PIZZEY, E. (1974) *Scream Quietly or the Neighbours Will Hear*, Penguin.

PRINGLE, M. K. (1978) 'The needs of abused children', in SMITH, S.M. (Ed.) *Maltreatment of Children*, MTP Press Ltd.

PRINGLE, M. K. (1975) *The Needs of Children*, Hutchinson, New York, Schocken.

PRINGLE, M. K. (1970) *Able Misfits*, Longman in association with National Children's Bureau.

RINGLER, N.M., KENNELL, J.H., JARVELLA, R., NAVOJOSKY, B.J. and KLAUS, M.H. (1975) 'Mother to child speech at 2 years: effects of early post-natal contact', *J. Paediatr*. 86, p. 141.

ROBERTS, J. (1978) 'Social work and child abuse', in MARTIN, J.P. (Ed.) *Violence and the Family*, John Wiley, New York.

ROGERS, D., TRIPP, J., BENTOVIM, A., ROBINSON, A., BERRY, A. and GOULDING, R. (1976) 'Non-accidental poisoning: an extended syndrome of child abuse', *B.M.J.*, April 13, pp. 793–6.

RUTTER, M. and MADGE, N. (Eds) (1976) *Cycles of Disadvantage*, Heinemann Educational.

SMITH, S.M. (1975) *The Battered Child Syndrome*, Butterworth.

STEELE, B. (1975) *Working with Abusive Parents from a Psychiatric Point of View*, U.S. Department of Health, Education and Welfare, Office of Child Development, OHO, pp. 75–70.

STRAUSS, P. and GIRODET, D. (1977) 'Three French follow-up studies of abused children', *Child Abuse and Neglect*, 1, pp. 99–103.

WOLKIND, S. (1977) 'Women who have been "in care" — psychological and social status during pregnancy', *Journal of Child Psychology and Psychiatry*, 18, 2, pp. 179–82.

Chapter 13

Towards the Prevention of Child Abuse*

Prevention must be based on three principles. First, that early action is likely to be less damaging and more effective than crisis intervention which by its very nature places a premium on speed rather than well-considered judgment. Second, that prevention must promote the best interests of the child rather than merely remove him/her from harmful experiences. When parental care is so damaging that alternative care has to be provided, then this must not only be better in the sense of being conducive to optimal development, but also therapeutic in the sense of healing the damage done, be it emotional, social, intellectual or physical. Otherwise there is a high risk of today's child becoming tomorrow's abusing parent.

Third, prior to an abused child being returned to his parents it is essential to apply very rigorous criteria to prevent re-injury or continued ill-treatment. On the basis of his own work, Kempe (Kempe and Kempe, 1978) suggests 'four objective changes' which need to have taken place: the abusive parent must have made at least one friend with whom he shares regular and enjoyable experiences; both parents must have found some-thing attractive in their abused child and be able to show it by talking lovingly, hugging or cuddling; both parents must have learned to use life-lines in moments of crisis; and brief reunions with their child must become increasingly enjoyable. If all four criteria are not met then, Kempe warns, it is premature to allow the child's return to his parents: 'he will be attacked again, and probably much more severely. Of course, it is very important to be sure that the reason for the family's improvement is not the absence of the child because, if so, his return will obviously reverse the process.'

Some may argue that not enough is known to prevent child abuse and that the results of further research must be awaited. However, in my view a

*This article originally appeared as Chapter 15 in Frude, N (Ed.) (1980) *Psychological Approaches to Child Abuse*, Batsford Academic and Educational.

simile from the medical field illustrates more accurately the present situation. Some years ago it became possible to vaccinate successfully against whooping cough or polio without understanding why a particular child was more liable to contract the disease or how to cure it. In the same way there is now a sufficient understanding of some of the broad preventive measures which could achieve a significant reduction in the incidence of child abuse. To bring this about, a major shift in public and professional attitudes must first take place.

Then the adoption of three measures would go a long way towards preventing child abuse. The first is the introduction of developmental checks for all children and a comprehensive assessment of every suspected case. The second is the provision of an independent voice for every child who is 'at risk'. The third, preparation for parenthood, is essentially a long-term measure.

Changing Professional and Public Attitudes

First and foremost it is essential that in all cases of abuse the balance should be tilted much more in favour of the child's interests and rights rather than those of the biological parents. This means making his/her long-term need for continuing, consistent and dependable loving care of paramount importance instead of, as at present, considering mainly the probability of future physical ill-treatment. When such care seems unlikely, then permanent separation or 'divorce' of the child from his family should become an option to be considered more frequently and earlier than is currently the case.

If psychological well-being were to be given equal weight with physical safety, then no child would be allowed to return to an environment where his all-round development would continue to be impeded or distorted. The criterion should be that a marked improvement has taken place, or can be expected with a high degree of confidence, in a previously damaging milieu. Clearly the more immature, disturbed or unstable the parents, and the more punitive or depriving their attitude to the child, the less realistic it is to expect such improvement. In these circumstances, the child's need for loving care should take precedence in law over the rights of the biological parents.

Professional attitudes need to change also in relation to the compulsory notification of child abuse; without it, the true incidence is unlikely ever to come to light. Resistance to this idea tends to be justified on the grounds of confidentiality, a breach of which, so it is argued, would damage the relationship of trust between a patient/client and his professional advisor. Yet recent evidence from New South Wales, Australia, might provide grounds for a reconsideration of this attitude. When a law was passed obliging doctors to report their suspicions, the number of known battered children tripled within twelve months.

A further change in professional attitudes relates to the need to shift the whole burden of responsibility for recognizing and dealing with abusing parents and abused children from social workers to a broadly based team drawn from many disciplines. In every case, at least a general practitioner, paediatrician, psychologist and a lawyer should be involved and often a health visitor, teacher, psychiatrist and police officer may also have to be brought in. Of course, these and other professional workers are already participating in case conferences but are less often directly responsible for the assessment, treatment and rehabilitation of every member of the family.

Both investigation and decision-making must in future become a truly shared task. Such sharing of responsibility seems essential not only because of the complex social and psychological factors underlying rejecting or violent parental behaviour, but also because no single profession can be expected either to have the necessary expertise or to bear unaided the strain involved in this work.

In addition to creating a climate of opinion which gives paramountcy to the interests of children, greater public awareness needs to be brought about regarding the likely incidence of child abuse. Few people realize that the present minimum estimate is that about 300 children in England and Wales are killed by their parents every year, about 3000 receive serious injuries (including permanent brain damage) and another 40,000 are victims of assault. The media have an influential and responsible part to play in changing people's reluctance to 'interfere'. Getting across the realization that the sheer survival of a small child may be at stake may make neighbours, shopkeepers and tradesmen prepared to convey what they know to someone with authority to investigate the situation.

Developmental Checks and Comprehensive Assessments

Regular developmental checks, at least for under-fives, have been shown by a large-scale French project, started ten years ago, to be a cost-effective undertaking (Strauss and Girodet, 1977). Handicaps are detected at an early stage and hence the need for lengthy hospital treatment is reduced. Cost-benefit studies also show that the earlier intervention and treatment take place, the lower the cost and the greater the benefits (Wynn, 1976). Because the youngest age group is the most vulnerable, their need for such checks is the greatest. If introduced as a universal service, it would in no way stigmatize families where there is the highest risk of child abuse.

Those of preschool age are at greatest risk because if ill-treated they can neither 'tell' nor even run away. Hence between birth and three years of age the checks should be at least once every six months, and then up to the age of five years at nine-monthly intervals.

To reduce costs, a first screening could be carried out by a health visitor. If there is any cause for anxiety, then a full developmental assessment should follow. This must be multi-disciplinary, covering all areas of growth. Hence both a paediatrician and a psychologist will be involved to begin with, then calling on other specialists as required.

Achieving Complete Coverage

Only by achieving near-complete coverage of all children can it be hoped to prevent or at least reduce the incidence of child abuse. One way of doing so would be to offer a special incentive payment to mothers who seek the required screening and full assessment when needed; however, economic considerations and possibly current public attitudes too, are likely to preclude the introduction of such a new benefit at present. An alternative would be to link developmental checks to the payment of family allowances. No doubt some will reject this suggested sanction as being unwarranted state intrusion into the privacy of family life. Critics may also argue that it is unnecessary to enforce developmental checks for all children when only a minority are likely to be either handicapped, rejected or abused. However, to judge from the French experience, this minority is very sizeable, at least one in three infants.

Others may fear that parents of poor children will be penalized because they may for a number of good reasons be unable to take them for regular checks. But these could take place in their own homes or in day-care facilities in which many of the most disadvantaged under-fives are placed. The number of health visitors would have to be considerably increased to make this possible. However, it would pay to do so since the hospital services required to treat handicapped and abused children are much more costly.

Parental right to privacy has to be balanced against another right which ought to concern society equally — the right of a child to loving care and protection both of his physical and mental health. After all, the state gives an allowance to parents in order to encourage good child care. Is it not common sense and good housekeeping to ensure that such care is in fact being provided? And if it is deficient, then to compensate for what is lacking or, if it is too damaging, then to find alternative care?

Comprehensive, Multi-disciplinary Assessments

Until regular and frequent developmental checks are available to all infants, it is essential that a comprehensive, multi-disciplinary assessment is undertaken in every suspected case of child abuse. Early warning signs must always be heeded to prevent more serious damage. Among these are 'failure to thrive', avoidance of eye contact and, when with adults, withdrawal, silence, lack of smiling, apparent distrust and 'frozen watchfulness'. Another sign is if a child's appearance, weight, behaviour and relationships improve on going to hospital or when placed in a foster home; then rejection or abuse should be suspected, since removing well-cared infants from familiar, secure surroundings has the opposite effect.

At present, there is a multiplicity of assessment services, located in hospitals, assessment centres of social services departments, in school psychological services and in child guidance clinics. This is not only wasteful, but not infrequently leads to expensive duplication. The manpower resources required for assessment are both highly skilled and expensive. Hence, almost by definition, they are likely to remain scarce. An amalgamation of these various services would not only be cost effective but might also be the first step in learning how to bring the various professions together in an interdependent, effective working relationship.

The child guidance service has for some years been under a cloud, with its long term future uncertain and controversial. Yet it is, and has been from the outset, a truly multi-disciplinary service where the basic team consists of a doctor, a psychologist and a social worker. This is not the place to consider why child guidance has become something of a backwater during the past ten years or so. It could, however, provide the prototype pattern for the assessment of all children whose development is causing concern, or who are considered to be 'at risk' — the socially disadvantaged, the educationally handicapped, those failing to thrive physically, children with physical or sensory handicap, the truant and delinquent, the emotionally disturbed child and those deprived of a normal family life who have to be received into care because their own parents are unable or unwilling to look after them. Among all these groups a proportion will be found to have been neglected, rejected or even abused by their parents or parent substitutes, either physically, psychologically or both.

The Role of the School

Once children go to school they come under the daily care of a trained professional person for a period of eleven years. Hence schools could potentially play a crucial role in prevention. Yet so far they have not done so in this country, unlike their American counterpart. There increasing participation has started to take place in recent years through a variety of child protection programmes involving both teachers and school children (Broadhurst, 1978). Partly as a result of this work, two-thirds of the cases of child abuse and neglect reported in 1975 were found to involve school children between the ages of five and seventeen years. This finding runs counter to the commonly accepted view that it is the under-fives, and young infants in particular, who are at greatest risk of abuse.

Further work is needed to reveal whether this is yet another undiscovered iceberg which comes to light only when the spotlight is turned on to older children. After all, a mere twenty-five years ago child abuse and the 'battered baby syndrome' were virtually unsuspected and unknown in the United States (Woolley and Evans, 1955; Kempe *et al.*, 1962). In this country, the fact that causes of multiple fractures of the long bones of infants and other injuries may be caused not by disease but by the violent actions of parents or other caregivers received attention even later (Griffiths and Moynihan, 1963; Cameron *et al.*, 1966).

Stemming from an increased involvement of schools in child abuse, most have reported a significant increase in the number of identified cases. 'Where schools have taken an active role in discovering and preventing child abuse and neglect, the result has been to help hundreds of families and children at risk. Each of them is a compelling reason for school systems everywhere to become involved' (Broadhurst, 1978). Surely this applies to Britain with equal force?

In fact in the case of Maria Colwell — the first to arouse public attention — a teacher was very aware of the child's rapid physical and mental deterioration and tried to get help for her. To enable teachers to play an active part in prevention, they would benefit from some inservice training so as to become more skilled in recognizing early warning signs and to know the courses of action open to them to protect the child.

'Child abuse, even if we exclude emotional deprivation, is a very widespread problem, and the consciousness is growing that traditional child-protection agences are simply not equal to it . . . they cannot possibly bring to bear all the skills this multifaceted problem requires. What is needed, and what is now beginning to be created, is a new and more broadly based approach that will draw more effectively on the resources of the community' (Kempe and Kempe, 1978).

An Independent Voice for the Child at Risk

'Many judges in Great Britain still demand the sorts of proof they would demand in a criminal case even in a civil case involving simply taking a child into care. For centuries the child has been a chattel in common law, and still today for many judges the rights of children are not yet nearly so important as the rights of parents'. This is the view of the foremost experts on child abuse (Kempe and Kempe, 1978). They argue that 'one radical but effective move to improve children's safety would be to make them full citizens, entitled to all rights except the vote.'

As recently as 1977, the Official Solicitor expressed the view that 'it is only in a minority of cases that the court would benefit from representation of a child's point of view by an advocate' (House of Commons, 1977). Though the House of Commons Select Committee accepted this view, at least it did recommend that 'the supervisor of an abused child should be given legal authority to visit the child or to obtain a medical examination'. Welcome though this recommendation is, it in no way affects what seems to me a strong case for giving all abused children the right to an independent spokesman who would ensure that their views and feeling are heard and taken into account.

At present, it is only in adoption proceedings that courts are required by statute to give consideration to the child's wishes; many of them are too young to make this a reality. In contrast, the age range of children who are abused or rejected, or involved in custody cases, spans the whole period of childhood right into adolescence. Paradoxically, these are denied the right to be heard and to have an independent spokesman.

A Small Step Forward

The 1975 Children Act takes a small step towards changing the situation, but it still has two serious drawbacks. First, when there is a potential conflict of interest between parent and child, courts are to have discretion to appoint an 'independent social worker' or solicitor or both to act for the child. But common sense and elementary justice demand that in all such situations the child's voice should be heard as of right. Hence this provision should be mandatory.

Secondly, an 'independent social worker' in this context means that he or she will be working for a different local authority from the one concerned with the parents and child. This seems unsatisfactory for a number of reasons. To start with, would not such a worker's first loyalty be (quite understandably) to his professional colleagues and, though to a lesser extent perhaps, to the viewpoint taken by another local authority? Next, I doubt whether hard-pressed social workers could take on this additional commitment on the scale required if all children in need were to be given a voice. Equally, if not more important, child care skills have, in my view, markedly declined during the past ten years, because of the change in social work ethos resulting from the Seebohm reorganisation.

Who then should undertake the role of spokesman? I see it as work akin to that being done by the Samaritans or Marriage Guidance Counsellors: a responsible job undertaken on behalf of the community by specially appointed lay people. In fact, a report from the Manchester Branch of the Samaritans in March, 1979, recorded that some 15 per cent of its 35,000 phone calls during 1978 were from children, some as young as eight years. This shows that even without a service specially designed to meet their needs, unhappy children are seeking adult support.

In order to provide an independent voice, a spokesman would require firsthand experience of children; some basic training in child development would also be essential. For particularly difficult cases (especially very young infants) the spokesman would need to call on the services of someone with a systematic and thorough knowledge of children's development and of how to observe and to communicate with them, such as child psychologists, paediatricians, child psychiatrists or those social workers who have specialized in this field.

What Difference Might a Spokesman Have Made to Maria Colwell?

By getting to know six-year old Maria while she was still living with her foster-parents, the spokesman would have seen a child well-loved by them and whom she loved in return; who was happy, well behaved, mixing normally with other children and making good progress at school. He would also have observed that when she was made to visit her mother's home Maria began to show clear signs of stress, and when she was made to stay overnight, she objected most strenuously and, in fact, ran away several times half-dressed and barefoot.

These signs the spokesman would have recognized as early warning signals of great strain and unhappiness. Nor would he have needed much skill to find out Maria's feelings since she was making them only too clear. But his training would have made him aware that running away, for example, is a much more serious symptom in a six than a thirteen-year-old, as is soiling by a child who had previously been clean.

Since the spokesman would be trying to see the situation through the child's eyes, determining what seemed in her best long-term interest, he would also have been given access to all the relevant background information. Knowing that Maria's foster parents had lovingly cared for her since babyhood would have ben as relevant as knowing that of her mother's nine children, six had been taken into care because of being neglected and had remained in care since early childhood, that during a recent three-year period the mother had had no fewer than nineteen different addresses, that the stepfather-to-be had several aliases and a criminal record including violence, and that her three children by him were not only often unkempt and dirty, but that neighbours were alleging they were being left alone at night.

Having discovered Maria's wishes, the spokesman's second task would have been to brief a lawyer on her behalf when the question of her care was being disputed in a court of law. Even if all the evidence had nevertheless failed to persuade the court to respect Maria's wish to remain with her foster-parents, the spokesman would still have been able to offer her some protection. For the third task of the spokesman would be to keep in touch with every child who is 'transplanted' from one family to another to ensure that the transplant has 'taken'. Also he would insist that there should be some continuity of contact with former parental figures and that contingency plans are available in case the transplant fails. The spokesman could meet these tasks only if he had the right to see the child alone, even if the 'new' parents denied access to their home. Had these principles been in force at the time, Maria might well be alive today.

It would have become quite evident to the spokesman after a short time that the 'transplant' was not succeeding. The dramatic deterioration of the child's physical and mental condition would have been a clear indication that something was going seriously wrong. Moreover, the spokesman would have been able to hear of Maria's distress from several other people. At least two teachers were deeply worried; several neighbours expressed their concern to the authorities on a number of occasions; and a local shop-keeper had objected so strongly to this small child having to heave heavy sacks of coal (equal to about two-thirds of her own weight) up the road to her home that she threatened to cease selling them unless Maria was given some sort of conveyance (an outsize pram was then provided by her mother).

In fact, Maria was to remain imprisoned (on occasions quite literally locked in a room) with people she had every reason to fear. She was forcibly restrained from ever seeing again the foster-parents she had loved and trusted for most of her life. And there was no one to whom she could even talk about them or about what was being done to her.

Within a period of fifteen months Maria changed from a happy, responsive, well-mannered child to being totally withdrawn, solitary, depressed, sitting for hours staring into space and not responding to children or adults. Clearly she was in a state of severe shock and deep mourning for the parents she had lost.

'Independent Social Workers'

Under new legislation which was enacted after Maria's death, she would have had as of right an 'independent social worker' to speak for her. But this would not necessarily have led to a different outcome because of two widely held social work tenets. One is that a child should wherever possible grow up with his or her biological family, since otherwise he or she would face an 'identity crisis' in adolescence. Yet there is little evidence that this is inevitably so. On the contrary, adoption provides vulnerable, and even damaged children with a second chance, even if they are placed with their new families long after infancy (Bohman, 1971; Kadushin, 1970; Seglow *et al.*, 1972). What is also well-documented is that children whose early life is extremely stressful and who fail to have mutually satisfying relationships with parental figures, become emotionally very vulnerable and prone to serious behaviour difficulties in later life.

The other belief is that stressing the importance of psychological rather than biological parents is a device for providing childless middle-class couples with children from inadequate working-class homes. In fact, this is a quite unwarranted slur on working-class families. It is exposed for the nonsense it is in Maria's case: her working-class foster-parents showed her the loving care and concern typical of the great majority of such parents.

Just as the 1975 Children Act made it possible to appoint an independent advocate for children caught in a 'tug-of-love' battle, whether between divorced parents, would-be adoptive parents, foster-parents or relatives, so a lay spokesman should be introduced and become mandatory for every abused child before the decision is taken whether he or she should return to those who have abused him or her.

The official Colwell report fails to make what seems to me a most significant point. Even if Maria had survived there would have been major, if not irreparable psychological scars resulting from the devastating damage to her emotional development. Actual battering is only the visible tip of the iceberg of emotional rejection and abuse, suffered daily by many thousands of children in this country. Surely a civilized society should strive to eliminate such suffering? A genuinely independent spokesman for children would be a first step in this direction.

Preparation for Parenthood

This is the third measure which is not only the most basic but also inevitably more long-term than the other two discussed previously. Its aim would be to raise the level of children's emotional, social and intellectual development in a way similar to that in which their physical health has been improved during the past forty years. The starting point would be the recognition that modern parenthood is too demanding and complex a task to be performed well merely because every adult has once been a child. Indeed it is about the only such skilled task for the performance of which no knowledge or training is expected or required. To improve the quality of family care, wide-ranging changes in the attitudes to parenthood and child rearing will have to be brought about (Pringle, 1975 and 1979).

Probably the most effective way would be to make available to all young people a programme of preparation for parenthood. What is required is neither a narrow course, seen as a branch of biology or home economics, nor a very wide general one in citizenship; the model of sex education is not appropriate either; nor should such a programme be confined to girls, and the less able ones at that, as tends to happen at present. Nor should such a programme be confined to schools.

Instead, a knowledge of human psychology would be the foundation and would include the dynamics of behaviour, the ways in which people interact and react at a great variety of levels, the role of values and the roots of prejudice. The opportunity to acquire a fairly sophisticated under-standing of the sequential nature of human development, of the various stages of physical and mental growth, of motivation and of the wide vari-ations in behaviour, including deviancy, would complement and supple-ment what children will have learnt already in their own homes.

Providing an Effective Programme

To be effective a programme of preparation for parenthood should have this broad base of human psychology and child development. Sex education, family planning, home economics and political education as well as first-hand practical experience of babies and young children would form an integral part of the programme.

Few schools do as yet provide such a broadly based scheme but the vast majority have for some time been offering their pupils sex education. With hindsight, this may have done more harm than good: an appropriate pers-pective on this topic is likely to be achieved only within the context of affectionate, mutually responsible relationships between the sexes rather than within the narrower biological setting of reproductive processes, child-birth, contraception and venereal diseases. Significantly enough, the need for a wider programme is well appreciated by young people themselves (Fogelman, 1976).

Developing programmes of preparation for parenthood in all schools would be a first step towards translating into practice the belief that children are society's seedcorn for the future. Concern for improving the quality of life must start with the young of today. To begin with, they should be helped to achieve a more realistic understanding of parenthood long before they decide whether or not to become parents. This should be based on an objective appreciation of its demands, constraints, satisfactions and challenges.

Home-making and parenting, especially motherhood, are simultaneously both under- and over-valued. On the one hand, the housewife with young children is described and treated as not being gainfully employed even though her working hours are usually twice as long as those of the 35-hour-a-week worker. On the other hand, an over-romanticized picture of motherhood prevails in our society, reinforced by the media.

Instead, a more truthful, even daunting, awareness needs to be created of the arduous demands which child-rearing makes not only on the emotions, energy and time, but also on financial resources. These are most actuely felt when the first baby comes along. The inevitable constraints on personal independence, freedom of movement and, indeed, one's whole way of life, require to be spelt out. Babies should be presented as they are, warts and all, rather than as heart-warmingly attractive, invariably sunny tempered with a dimply, angelic smile.

For this realistic portrayal to be believed, it must be seen to be true — hence the importance of first-hand experience with babies and young children. There are many different ways in which this could be provided. What is vital is that it should be viewed in the same way as laboratory work in chemistry or physics — work to be done regularly for a considerable period of time. In this way, the physical care required by babies and toddlers will also come to be appreciated more realistically than by using dolls as models.

Family Planning — Age and Size

Postponing parenthood until both partners are fully mature is in the best interest not only of their own long-term relationship but also of their future child. Similarly, family planning can be linked with the concept that responsible parenthood means having only as many children as a couple can emotionally tolerate and financially afford. This fact is demonstrated by evidence showing that in general children from large families are at a disadvantage physically, educationally and in terms of social adjustment.

Family size begins to exert an unfavourable influence right from birth onwards, high perinatal mortality being associated with high parity. Nor is it solely a question of low income and thus a lower standard of living: effects of family size upon development operate irrespective of social class. When parental time, attention, and maybe also patience, have to be shared, then less is available for each child. Thus large families put a strain on both financial and psychological resources. The fact that some parents successfully rear large families does not invalidate the general picture.

Promoting and Supporting Good Parenting

Preparation for parenthood in one sense starts at birth since a child learns about it through his own experience of family life. However, those deprived of adequate parental care have little chance of becoming in turn responsible parents themselves. In any case, it might raise both the status and the level of parenting if the total population were to receive some direct preparation for the task. The earliest, and in a sense best, opportunity to achieve this occurs with school children because they are a captive audience.

To be fully effective, subsequent opportunities must continue to be available for young people, including couples expecting their first child, to prepare themselves for parenthood. Youth organizations, centres for further and adult education, advice and counselling services for young people as well as pregnancy advisory, maternity and marriage guidance services, all have a part to play in this task (Pugh, 1979). If such opportunities became freely and readily available, then the parental life style may come to be chosen more deliberately in the fuller realization of its responsibilities and satisfactions.

Abstaining from Violence against Children

Perhaps child abuse and its prevention ought to be considered within the wider context of physical chastisement. In this country it is practised against children both by their parents and those standing *in loco parentis* as a means of 'disciplining' them. Teachers are most likely to use an instrument, such as the cane or tawse, for corporal punishment and it is most frequently employed in secondary schools. Some 80 per cent do so to a greater or lesser extent (Fogelman, 1976). In contrast, parents are more likely to use a hand only and to punish younger children. However, as many as 62 per cent of parents were found to smack their one-year-olds and 93 per cent their four-year-olds, 17 per cent of whom were smacked at least once a day (Newson and Newson, 1968).

Yet surely it is generally accepted that the aim of discipline — if it is to be effective — must lead to self-discipline and self-control. Physical punishment is therefore ineffective in a number of ways. To begin with, it produces modified behaviour mainly while the threat of being observed or discovered is present. Next, it primarily promotes greater ingenuity so as to avoid being detected. That its effect in changing behaviour is limited, is demonstrated by the fact that all too often the same pupils are repeatedly punished; some of them may even come to be regarded as heroes by their fellows because of their ability to withstand beatings. Any deterrent effect on others — again only while the threat is present — is likely to be outweighed by the feelings of hostility, particularly in the more thoughtful and sensitive, aroused by witnessing the indignity inflicted time and again on their classmates.

Research confirms (Fogelman, 1976) that corporal punishment is disliked by children and young people, contrary to the assertions of the opposite by its supporters. Last, but by no means least, it is to some extent even counter-productive since it teaches the child an unintended but nonetheless obvious lesson that 'might is right' and hence if you are bigger you can intimidate and hit those smaller or weaker than yourself. Conversely, children are better behaved in schools where corporal punishment is not used (Rutter *et al.*, 1979).

As a society we now disapprove of violence against the person and express particular disapproval of violent behaviour by children. Also all forms of physical punishment have now been abolished by law in the armed forces, in prisons, borstals and detention centres. So is it not illogical as well as unjust that there is such general acceptance of corporal punishment of children? Is it not hypocritical to condemn their physical aggression when we practise it on them as a matter of course and disingenuous when we profess to set children an example of how to behave by the way we ourselves do? And is such a climate of opinion not bound to reduce the threshold at which parents are prepared to use grave physical violence against even quite young babies?

Anyone training dogs or other animals knows that the infliction of pain is not a good method of bringing about desired behaviour — why then do we continue to believe it to be so in relation to the human young? Moreover, in our society people consume a vast array of medicines and drugs in an endeavour to escape discomfort and pain. Why then do we continue to cling to the belief that pain inflicted on the young is educative and morally reforming?

Maybe child abuse will only be eradicated when we determine that the time has come to condemn and abstain from all physical punishment of children as we have for so many years now abolished its use against adults.

References

BOHMAN, M. (1971) 'A comparative study of adopted children, foster children and children in their biological environment born after undesired pregnancies', *Acta Paediatrica Scandinavica*, Supplement No. 3221.

BROADHURST, D.D. (1978) 'What schools are doing about child abuse and neglect', *Children Today*, 7, pp. 22–36.

CAMERON, J.M., JOHNSON, J.R.M. and CAMPS, F.E. (1966) 'The battered child syndrome', *Medicine, Science and the Law*, 6, pp. 2–21.

Department of Health and Social Security (1974) *Report of the Committee of Inquiry into the Care and Supervision Provided in Relation to Maria Colwell*, HMSO, London.

FOGELMAN, K. (Ed) (1976) *Britain's Sixteen Year Olds*, National Children's Bureau, London.

GRIFFITHS, D.L. and MOYNIHAN, F.J. (1963) 'Multiple epiphyseal injuries in babies (battered baby syndrome)', *British Medical Journal*, No. 5372, pp. 1558–61.

House of Commons (1977) *Violence to Children, First Report for the Select Committee on Violence in the Family*, HMSO, London.

JOBLING, M. (1976) *The Abused Child: An Annotated Bibliography*, National Children's Bureau, London.

KADUSHIN, A. (1971) *Adopting Older Children*, Columbia University Press, New York.

KEMPE, R.S. and KEMPE, C.H. (1978) *Child Abuse*, Fontana/Open books, London.

KEMPE, C.H., SILVERMAN, F., STEELE, B., DROEGMUELLER, W., and SILVER, H. (1962) 'The battered child syndrome', *Journal of the American Medical Association*, 181, pp. 17–24.

NEWSON, J. and NEWSON, E. (1968) *Four Years Old in the Urban Community*, Allen and Unwin, London.

PRINGLE, M.K. (1975) *The Needs of Children*, Hutchinson, London.

PRINGLE, M.K. (1979) *A Fairer Future*, Macmillan, London.

PUGH, G. (1979) *Preparation for Parenthood: Some Current Initiatives*, National Children's Bureau, London.

RUTTER, M., MAUGHAN, B., MORTIMORE, R. and OUSTON, J. (1979) *15,000 Hours: Secondary Schools and their Effects on Children*, Open Books, London.

SEGLOW, J., PRINGLE, M.K. and WEDGE, P. (1972) *Growing Up Adopted*, NFER, Slough.

STRAUSS, P. and GIRODET, D. (1977) 'Three French follow-up studies of abused children', *Child Abuse and Neglect*, 1, pp. 99–103.

WOOLLEY, P.V. and EVANS, W.A. (1955) 'The significance of skeletal lesions in infants resembling those of traumatic origin', *Journal of the American Medical Association*, 158, pp. 539–43.

WYNN, A. (1976) 'Health care systems for preschool children', *Proceedings of the Royal Society of Medicine*, 69, pp. 340–43.

Chapter 14

The Roots of Violence and Vandalism*

Introduction

The topic of motivation and causation is so complex that I can only touch on some of the major issues. I shall concentrate on preventive measures, since prevention is always better than cure. Better, not only because the time and skill of the police force could be employed on more important matters, once the incidence of vandalism and violence has been reduced; but better also, I would guess, in terms of cost effectiveness. So it is in everyone's interest to support not only short-term ways of combating them, but also preventive measures even though they are inevitably long-term.

What follows is based on research results, both other people's and that of the National Children's Bureau. I will not quote detailed results or statistics since these are available in published form. There are three questions I shall discuss. First, what are the roots of violence and vandalism? Second, if there has been an increase in recent years, what might be the reasons? And third, what measures might be taken to reduce their incidence?

The Roots of Violence and Vandalism

As with most human behaviour, there is unlikely to be a single or simple reason, but rather several, and often complex causes. Violence and vandalism are probably linked to the most basic emotional needs and the extent to which these are met or remain unfulfilled.

---

*Based on an address given at the invitation of the Association of Municipal Corporations, the County Councils Association, and the Association of Chief Police Officers this paper was published in *Concern*, 11, 1972–3, pp. 17–24; *Community Schools Gazette*, 66, 7, 1972, pp. 325–32; *Therapeutic Education*, 1, 1, 1973, pp. 3–11; *Virginia Journal of Education*, 69, 5, 1976, pp. 17–21; and as a separate pamphlet by the NCB.

I find a fourfold classification of these needs useful, though many people prefer considerably longer lists. They are: the need for love and security; for new experiences; for praise and recognition; and for responsibility. These needs have to be met from the very beginning of life and continue to require fulfilment — to a greater or lesser extent — until the end of life.

If one of these basic needs remains unmet — or inadequately met — then one of two reactions follows: fight or flight, attack or withdrawal. Society reacts much more strongly to those children and young adults who respond by fighting, attacking — probably because this is seen as a challenge to authority; because it arouses feelings of aggression and revenge; and because by force we can control its outward expression, at least temporarily. But there is little evidence that meeting aggression with coercion brings about any lasting change; rather, a vicious circle is set up — with escalating violence and inevitably more forceful control.

The Need for Love and Security

This need is probably the most important one. It is the basis of all later relationships, not only within the family, but with friends, colleagues and eventually one's own family. On it depend the healthy development of the personality, the ability to care and respond to affection and, in time, to become a loving, caring parent. This need is met by the child's experiencing from birth onwards a continuous, reliable, loving relationship — first with his mother, then father and then an ever-widening circle of adults and contemporaries.

When it is not met adequately, then the consequences are pretty disastrous later on, both for the individual and for society. Our prisons, mental hospitals, borstals and schools for the maladjusted, contain a high proportion of individuals who in childhood were unloved and rejected; their number is high too among the chronically unemployable and among what I have termed 'able misfits'. Anger, hate and lack of concern for others are common reactions to being unloved and rejected. Vandalism and violence are an expression of these feelings. This same reaction can be seen in embryo, when a young child who has been scolded or smacked, goes and kicks his doll, or the dog, or a table.

Through a loving relationship, children learn to control their anger or to use it constructively; without affection, it remains primitive, and grows more vicious and vengeful with increasing physical strength.

The Need for New Experiences

Only if this need is adequately met throughout childhood and adolescence, will a child's intelligence develop fully. Just as the body needs food for physical development and just as an appropriate balanced diet is essential for normal growth, so new experiences are for the mind.

To the baby, everything is an exciting new experience; watching his own fingers, listening to a watch, taking his first steps. In later years, the challenge will be learning to master reading or riding a bicycle or climbing a mountain. In adulthood, new experiences come through work or leisure; watching a football match, buying a new hat or writing a book, remain exciting experiences right into old age.

The more uneventful and dull life is, the more we become bored, frustrated and restless. This is shown clearly by the contrast between the eagerness, alertness and vitality of normal babies whose life is filled with new experiences and challenges; and the aimlessness and boredom of the adolescent with nothing to do and nowhere to go. In seeking — legitimately — for the excitement of new experiences, where few are to be found or attainable, the forbidden, risky or dangerous are liable to acquire an aura of daring and excitement. What may start as a lark — an expression of high spirits and the desire for adventure — can turn into vandalism and violence. This happens all the more readily, the longer and the more pervasive the boredom and frustration of their lives.

One outstanding fact is that violence and vandalism are predominantly male activities. Why should this be so? One explanation may be that boys and men have a greater desire, perhaps even need, for experiences which are challenging or dangerous. Another is that physical punishment and violence are more often meted out to boys than girls, which is likely in turn to provoke aggressiveness and violence.

The Need for Praise and Recognition

To grow from a helpless baby into a self-reliant adult requires an immense amount of emotional, social and intellectual learning. It is accomplished by the child's modelling himself on the adults who are caring for him. The most effective incentives to bring this about — which requires a continuous effort, sustained throughout the years of growing up — are praise and recognition. Eventually, a job well done becomes its own reward but that is a very mature stage; and even the most mature adult responds and indeed blossoms, when given — at least occasionally — some praise or other form of recognition.

Unfortunately, we give praise and recognition to achievement and not to effort. In consequence, this need is readily and often satisfied in the case of intelligent, healthy, adjusted and attractive children. In contrast, the intellectually slow, the culturally disadvantaged, the emotionally deprived or disturbed, get far less, if any, praise and recognition. Yet their need is very much greater. Whatever small successes they have, inevitably demand much effort and perseverance; yet they receive less reward because they achieve less. Worse still, those who are rejected by their parents, and regarded as failures by their teachers, are wholly deprived of the satisfaction of this need by adults.

The only avenue open to them is to win the admiration and recognition of their mates. Being accepted as a member of a gang, or better still becoming its leader, is one means of achieving this. Then, it is not too big a step to vandalism and violence: showing off, doing something 'for a dare', behaving in a way the individual would not do by himself but is enabled to by being carried along by the contagious excitement and 'safety' of a group — all these are characteristic of gangs; and 'able misfits' — rejected, affectionless youngsters, whose ability is unrecognized — may be the 'brains' behind the exploits.

The Need for Responsibility

To begin with, this need is met through having possessions, however small and inexpensive, over which the child is allowed to exercise absolute ownership. As he gets older, responsibility has to be extended to more important areas, including being gradually granted responsibility and freedom over his own actions. Eventually, in full maturity, he should be able to accept responsibility for others.

Like all skills, it needs to be practised and exercised under adult guidance which should diminish as the child grows into adolescence and adulthood. The child who is denied opportunities to exercise responsibility will fail to develop a sense of responsibility for himself, for others or for material objects. The upbringing of such children, also, often lacks training in self-control, in waiting and working for what they want, and in treasuring their own and other people's property. In consequence, such young people tend to be impulsive, unwilling (and unable in some cases) to postpone the immediate gratification of their impulses, and contemptuous of the rights of others. Among them one would expect a high degree of vandalism and violence.

Later on, employment plays a vital part. Work which makes little demand on the need for responsibility and involvement, is likely to enhance further the sense of alienation and irresponsibility, which is bred by being made to feel an educational and vocational reject. Repetitive, boring and mentally (as well as often physically) undemanding work is undoubtedly linked with young workers' craving to find, in their spare time, excitement and an outlet for bottled-up energies. In our society the opportunity to work plays an important part in self-respect yet technical advances, together with automation, are making even undemanding jobs scarce; for example, fork-lift trucks can do the work of ten employees in a warehouse. Hence opportunities for unskilled teenagers have greatly diminished. Also unemployment has hit the less able, more educationally backward school leaver. Enforced idleness, boredom and little money in his pocket tend to undermine further what little self-respect is left to the adolescent who has for years been caught in a web of multiple disadvantages. Feeling that society disowns him, may well engender a feeling that he in turn owes nothing to society.

Are Vandalism and Violence Increasing, and If So, Why?

The answer to the first part of the question is not in fact straightforward. An apparent statistical increase may be due to changes in practice of reporting or recording. And what is the baseline in making comparisons? Ten, twenty or fifty years? Two quotations will illustrate my point: 'The art of crime has increased faster than the art of detection' (1828 Select Committee — in *A History of Criminal Law, Vol. 4*, by Radzinowics). The second quote: 'Today almost every institution which has served man during the past few centuries is on trial. The values of the last generation seem as remote as the Stone Age. The spirit of criticism and dissatisfaction permeates the social fabric and invades the domain of morals and conduct' (*Times Educational Supplement*, April 1920).

Even if there has been an increase, there are many conditions in present-day society likely to be causing it. To mention a few: redevelopment, high density urban living and job mobility, have torn communities apart and led to a more impersonal environment for young people. Did being known by sight at least to neighbours, tradesmen and the local bobby, impose some restraint? There is evidence from animal studies that both overcrowding and noise lead to violent and destructive behaviour. May not the same be true of us? Children and young people are now physically healthier and stronger, and hence have more energy. Do we provide sufficient outlets for it? The age group twelve to twenty-seven years — which perhaps causes most concern, is the post-war (1945–1960) generation of the A bomb, H bomb and other extremely powerful destructive devices. Is there a link between these terrible, impersonal weapons, the open display of brutality and violence in the mass media and entertainment, and an increase in violence and vandalism? What are the effects on young minds of the instant and constant portrayal of violence in our daily papers and TV news bulletins?

Last, but by no means least, today's greater general affluence may make relative deprivation more difficult to bear: when the ownership of material possessions is widely advertised and equated with the good life; when having fun at parties, on yachts and at exotic beaches abroad, is featured prominently as the desirable way to spend one's leisure; then is it not likely that the dull, dead streets of inner cities and of suburbia as well as the windy deserts below vast high-rise towers, feel even duller, deader and more frustrating by comparison? When everyone is poor or in danger, a shared fate makes for fellow feeling and solidarity. The more glaring the inequalities, the greater the resentment and hostility.

What Measures Might Reduce Vandalism and Violence?

The most obvious solutions may seem to be greater protection of property; more policemen; and more severe punishment. If what I have tried to argue is accepted — that vandalism and violence are symptoms — then the underlying causes need to be tackled as well. Doing so would be more economical because, in the long run, more effective. The protective measures taken by the council of just one medium-sized city to guard its schools cost £2000 a month; even so, vandals will do damage elsewhere, for which the local community will pay one way or another.

Some measures for reducing the incidence of vandalism and violence are suggested again in relation to the four basic emotional needs.

The Need for Love and Security

Only really long-term measures have any chance of success here. Basically, we must develop a similar concern for children's emotional, social and intellectual development as we now have for their physical health. This requires a wide dissemination of what is known about the needs and stages of normal child development — in short, preparation of young people for parenthood. This is when real 'prevention' starts — with future parents.

'Being wanted and loved' may well be the most important factor in giving a child a good chance in life. The incidence of vandalism and violence would be significantly reduced, if the slogan 'every child a wanted child' became a reality. Appropriate moral and social education of tomorrow's parents could hasten the day when society really cares for the children it chooses to have. It has been said that a country gets the government it deserves. I think it is even more true that it gets the children it deserves.

The Need for New Experiences

Opportunities, both at school and for leisure activities, are vital here. Secondary schools, in particular, need to reform their curricula and organization to become more appropriate and relevant to the twenty per cent least academically able or interested pupils. Again, difficulties start early and, without special attention, grow worse as time goes on. For example, the Bureau's National Child Development Study shows that, even at the age of seven years, disadvantaged children from socially deprived homes are educationally severely retarded and emotionally disturbed. By adolescence, the degree of truancy, delinquency and vandalism is high among such children.

Research has shown that schools which attempt to give each pupil a sense of belonging, which do not stream and do not use corporal punishment, have a lower incidence of bullying, violence and delinquency. Another measure which has proved successful is to provide interesting activities during the holidays, based on schools; the cost of this is more than met by the reduction of damage to premises caused by vandalism.

Disadvantaged children all too often go to disadvantaged schools and also have very few opportunities for satisfying leisure activities. In any case, the youth service is woefully inadequate, fragmented and — by and large — far too conventional in the activities it offers. Thus, it is quite unable to attract those youngsters most in need of somewhere to go and something exciting to do. The thousands who flock to pop festivals clearly demonstrate this. For some young people, such schemes as 'outward bound', police or fire brigade cadets, have much to offer. Many others, however, crave the excitement of, say, racing — be it go-karts, motor bikes or cars — or the physical test of boxing, judo or wrestling. Street corner clubs and clubs which are prepared to replace traditional activities by those chosen by the young people themselves, readily attract members, even in high-need urban areas. This has been found in an experimental action-project the Bureau is carrying out in seven areas in collaboration with local authority family advice services into intermediate treatment facilities for children in trouble.

The Need for Praise and Recognition

Some of the measures just outlined, would in themselves provide a sense of achievement, and hence recognition. Also, we must learn to give praise not only to actual achievement but to effort — be it at school, work or leisure. Otherwise, the less able and the more disadvantaged will opt out of what to them is an unequal struggle.

In our competitive society, exams and certificates have almost become the hallmark of success; not only for climbing up the economic ladder but in finding employment, when the need for unskilled labour is contracting. Remedial education schemes and specially designed further education and training facilities are essential. To provide these in approved schools, borstals and prisons should be an essential part of the 'cure', but earlier preventive provision would be both cheaper and more effective.

Young people also need to become involved in their own communities. Again, the Bureau has found that this is possible, even in apparently most unpromising areas. In the project just mentioned, young people helped, for example, to clear a bombed site and make it into an adventure playground for preschool children.

Of course, if too much is expected too soon, failure and further frustration are certain. Progress will be slow, uncertain and erratic; but there will be none, unless praise and recognition are granted for even the smallest step forward.

The Need for Responsibility

How can one grant responsibility to the irresponsible? This is indeed a problem. There is no way out of the dilemma that, unless you are given it, you cannot learn how to exercise it. Some schools who cater for deprived, disturbed or delinquent youngsters have shown that it is worth taking the risks involved.

There are rarely dramatic or quick improvements. But if some of the measures suggested to meet the other emotional needs are taken, then this need too will be met. For example, the young people who cleared the site for a playground were quite affronted when it was damaged by vandals. Yet not so long ago they themselves would have acted in the self-same way.

Quite spontaneously they repaired the damage: then they took steps to protect the site from further damage.

Will-power or Determinism?

Stressing the importance of these basic psychological needs, inevitably raises two questions; if they remain unfulfilled, is a child doomed forever? And, if he is not, what determines whether or not he succeeds in overcoming the ill-effects of early deprivation? At present, no precise answers are available to this vital question; in fact, opinions cover the whole range from determinism, to the belief that everyone, given the will, can 'win through'.

The advocates of determinism run the risk of conveying to young people that a deprived early life is an excuse, indeed almost a justification for subsequent violence and lawlessness. Although this attitude is unwarrantably defeatist, nevertheless no-one is entirely 'master of his fate', least of all those who — even from before birth — have been beset by a pattern of complex and continuing disadvantage; to them, this assertion has a hollow, hypocritical ring.

The truth may lie somewhere between the two extreme positions. In any case, in practice we cannot but act as if it were never too late, as if rehabilitation and treatment always have a chance of success. Otherwise we give up hope which is a sure recipe for failure.

Conclusion

This paper tried to show that vandalism and violence are among the consequences of failing to meet children's basic emotional needs. This belief has two major practical implications: the first relates to ends, the second to means. In the past thirty years, a revolution has been brought about in the health and physical development of children by applying new medical and scientific measures. In the next thirty years, a similar revolution could, I believe, be brought about in their mental health, by applying new social, psychological and educational knowledge. This must start even before the child is born, otherwise 'equality of opportunity' will remain an illusion; and among the symptoms of deprivation and rejection, will continue to be vandalism and violence.

Secondly, with regard to means, no one professional group, or government department — local or central — has the key. Health, housing, social and educational measures must all combine to seek solutions to poverty and to multiple deprivation. What is needed is a kind of inter-professional combined operation. The promotion of this inter-disciplinary approach is, in fact, one of the chief aims of the National Children's Bureau, which hopes to have wide support in its efforts to increase as well as to apply available knowledge of human conduct. The more successfully society assists youth to maturity and to prefer acceptable alternatives to violence and vandalism, the fewer resources will need to be diverted to the task of dealing with them.

Though a good deal is already known, much remains to be learned about how best to achieve these goals. A variety of strategies will have to be explored: for promoting optimal emotional and intellectual development; for preventing deprivation, particularly during the most important early years of childhood; and, most difficult of all, for breaking into the vicious circle of the emotionally and intellectually deprived children of today becoming tomorrow's parents of yet another generation of deprived children.

References

BONE, M. and ROSS, E. (1972) *The Youth Service and Similar Provision for Young People*, H.M.S.O.
CRELLIN, E., PRINGLE, M.K. and WEST, P. (1971) *Born Illegitimate*, N.F.E.R.
DAVIE, R., BUTLER, N.R. and GOLDSTEIN, H. (1972) *From Birth to Seven*, Longman.
EWEN, J. (1972) *Towards a Youth Policy*, M.B.S. Publications.
GREER, C. (1972) *The Great School Legend*, Basic Books, U.S.A.
LEISSNER, A. (1969) *Street Club Work in Tel Aviv and New York*, Longman.
LEISSNER, A., HERDMAN, A. and DAVIES, E. (1971) *Advice, Guidance and Assistance*, Longman.
PRINGLE, M.K. (1969) *Caring for Children*, Longman.
PRINGLE, M.K. (1970) *Able Misfits*, Longman.
PRINGLE, M.K. (1971, 2nd ed.) *Deprivation and Education*, Longman.
ROSS, J.M., BUNTON, W.J., EVISON, P. and ROBERTSON, T.S. (1972) *A Critical Appraisal of Comprehensive Education*, N.F.E.R.

Chapter 15

Intermediate Treatment: An Overview*

'What is intermediate treatment?' is a question often put by the intelligent layman who happens to come across the term; but it is also asked by many professional workers — other than social workers — who are concerned with children and young people, in particular teachers and doctors. Admittedly, it was coined relatively recently, appearing first in the 1968 White Paper *Children in Trouble*[1] and being then built into the 1969 Children and Young Persons Act[2].

The roots of the concept, however, go back much farther. They grew from child care policies which increasingly emphasized the need for early preventive measures and for relinquishing the unreal distinction between deprived, disadvantaged and delinquent children. Compensation for inimical personal, family and environmental circumstances came to be seen as more appropriate than punishment. Intermediate treatment was conceived as a form of intervention halfway between removing a delinquent child from his family and neighbourhood on the one hand; and on the other hand, letting him remain at home under supervision. It was also intended to be a preventive measure for those 'at risk' of becoming delinquent. In fact an integral component of intermediate treatment was to avoid the segregation of young offenders by allowing them to participate in programmes which included children in the community who had not come before the courts.

Non-institutional Intervention

Disenchantment with residential types of provision has become evident in many different contexts. Long-stay hospitals for the mentally or physically handicapped; boarding schools for maladjusted children; residential nurseries and children's homes for those needing substitute family care; all of

*First published in *Concern*, 24, 1977, pp. 6–11.

137

these have come to be regarded as being less desirable, less viable and less constructive alternatives to living within a family and community setting.

In addition to the danger of institutions 'institutionalizing' both inmates and staff, residential settings are now seen to have other disadvantages and shortcomings. For one thing, they are ever more costly to run. Next it is difficult to staff them because in a relatively affluent society, which no longer has a surplus of single women willing to devote themselves to this kind of work, residential life has little appeal. Moreover, it is now recognized that such work needs not only dedication but highly skilled trained staff if it is to play its proper role of treatment, rehabilitation and restoration to the community wherever possible; yet the proportion of trained workers is dismally low.

In relation to juvenile delinquents, the disenchantment with residential provision has been further increased by the apparently falling 'success rate'. From an unsatisfactory rate of about 50 per cent twenty years ago, it had dropped still further by the mid 1960s to about 38 per cent. Considering that the definition of success is itself far from positive — merely that the delinquent has not been found guilty of an offence within three years of discharge — it was perhaps inevitable that new hopes should be pinned on non-institutional forms of intervention for those 'in trouble'. A further factor was the recognition of the positive power of parental and community involvement.

The attractive slogan 'community care' has, however, far too often remained an empty catchphrase because the necessary supportive, rehabilitative and treatment services have not been provided. Yet the more disadvantaged the child and his family and the more deprived the locality, the more essential such services are. Without them, the concept of community care is in danger of being rejected as having failed when in truth it has not been given a proper chance to succeed. This applies as much to intermediate treatment as it does to urban aid, to educational priority areas and to all other measures of positive discrimination. If no additional resources are provided or are made available on too limited a scale, or for too short a period, then the inevitably disappointing results lead to a condemnation of what could have been viable schemes.

Intermediate Treatment — Definition and Aims

The most recent definition has been put forward by a working group set up by the Personal Social Services Council under my chairmanship[3]. 'Intermediate treatment is action through a range of community-based programmes planned to meet identified needs of children and young persons who are at risk of appearing or who have appeared before the courts.' It was seen as encompassing a preventive role for disadvantaged young people; as a provision for those at risk of coming before the courts as well as those who have already been before the courts and placed on a supervision order; and for those in care, whether living in a community or foster home. In addition, a more 'intensive' form of intermediate treatment is being proposed in the report for the small minority who are more seriously and persistently delinquent.

The aims of intermediate treatment were seen by the working group as being threefold: 'to reduce delinquent behaviour and prevent new involvement in antisocial behaviour; to reduce the need for institutional care; and to prevent the inappropriate placement of a child or young person in a residential establishment.' The underlying assumption is that through improving a child's self-esteem, social skills, level of educational attainments and ability to make relationships while at the same time offering satisfying alternatives to crime, he will become less involved in delinquency which in turn will reduce the need for institutional care.

The Bureau's own report on intermediate treatment published in March of this year[4] offered a somewhat different definition. It was seen as a 'range or combination of programmes aimed at bridging the gap between the two extremes of compulsory removal of the young person from his family and community, and of leaving him in his environment without any controls or treatment provisions.' The aims were to provide new interests and experiences 'which can counteract, and provide alternatives to, delinquent or other undesirable influences and involvements . . . This approach seeks to prevent those segregating and labelling processes which are in themselves causal factors in the emergence and perpetuation of delinquent sub-cultures.' While specific provision may have to be made for individuals with special needs and problems, this is done within the wider context of a range of programmes accessible to and hence benefitting all the children and young people in the neighbourhood.

Community participation in the planning and provision of such services is seen as an integral aspect of this approach. This means enlisting the involvement of the parents as well as of other adults while simultaneously fostering the involvement of the youngsters themselves in the life of their community. To set up and run playgroups, adventure playgrounds, arts centres, sports programmes, discotheques and the like, required the mobilization of a wide range of community resources through the mediation of professional workers. Through being based on Family Advice Centres, it became possible to interlink these activities and services. For example, a mother may seek 'advice, guidance and assistance' for a personal problem; she then becomes active in organizing a mothers-and-babies group; this group in turn decides to provide a recreational programme for old-age pensioners of the neighbourhood; the senior citizens on their part then help to raise funds for a school holiday programme for local youngsters and a number of these young people start a window cleaning and decorating service for the old people while others get drawn into building a playground for the younger children.

Distinguishing Features of Intermediate Treatment Programmes

So far, none of the distinguishing features of intermediate treatment programmes are new or unique in themselves. Rather it is their flexibility, variety, comprehensiveness and, at best, multidisciplinary, cooperative nature, which is or should be their main characteristic. It could be argued with some justification that it is little more than what caring, educated parents provide for their growing children in order to broaden their horizons, widen their range of new experiences so as to stimulate their intellectual curiosity about the world, and to deepen their ability to make relationships with an ever-increasing range of people.

Perhaps it is a reflection of how demanding, skilled and challenging the job of good parenting is that when it has to be complemented or supplemented by professionals, no single discipline or service is capable of providing all that is required. To be effective, social workers, probation officers, youth workers, teachers, instructors, artists, magistrates and the police need to be involved in intermediate treatment; both statutory services and voluntary organizations have a vital part to play; and a substantial contribution could be made by volunteers. Yet none of these can or should usurp completely the parental role. For this reason and also because the parents' attitude to the adolescent inevitably remains a major influence, their agreement to, and wherever possible active involvement in, intermediate treatment programmes must be sought. Indeed it could be argued that inability or refusal to give support and to participate, might be seen as contra-indications to the suitability of community-based, intermediate treatment.

At its simplest, intermediate treatment provides challenging or exciting activities to counter the boredom which afflicts the life of many inner city youngsters with little to do (legitimately that is) and nowhere to go (without infringing someone else's privacy or property). Also, because many disadvantaged children and young people have a poor self-image compounded by educational failure and lack of opportunity to try their hand at new types of activities, intermediate treatment programmes endeavour to provide such opportunities in the fields of sport, games, crafts, the arts — whether acting, painting or learning to play an instrument — and hobbies of various kinds; in every case the emphasis is on active participation with the aim of fostering the individual's skills and self-confidence.

In addition to such programmes, which are primarily activity-based, intermediate treatment must also provide the opportunity for those who have been emotionally and socially deprived, to make supportive and dependable personal relationships. This is possible through sharing interests and activities with like-minded groups led by experienced youth workers. Some young people, however, require a one-to-one relationship, in some cases because having lacked this experience, they are too demanding or too withdrawn in group situations, while in the case of others, disruptive behaviour can be dealt with more effectively when individual attention is available.

Providing such close personal attachments presents difficulties in terms of professional staff but volunteers could play a much bigger part than they do at present. How successfully this can be done and on how large a scale has been shown by the successful recruitment of 'lay people', i.e., those who are not trained teachers, in the Adult Literacy Scheme. Of course, adequate support, guidance and supervision must be provided and professional resources are also essential for the recruitment and allocation of volunteers to individual children and young people, so that the latter's needs can be matched by the former's interests, skills and personality.

There are two further components of intermediate treatment which have remained so far underdeveloped and hence relatively little used. These are community service and restitution for damage done. Again there is much that can be learnt from the success in the adult field of Community Service Orders for offenders as an alternative to prison sentences. Though only introduced as recently as 1972, they have already become a widely accepted measure. In contrast, work in the service of the community and repayment, as it were, for damage inflicted on the community, have not at present established themselves as a part of community-based care for children and young people.

Yet there are several reasons why their widespread introduction could not only make an additional contribution to the range of available options but why they would also enhance the credibility, and hence acceptance, of the intermediate treatment concept. Among them are the fact that it would defuse the jibe that it is 'merely treats not treatment'. It would make it more acceptable to magistrates, many of whom so far remain sceptical of its value. The adolescent would be offered a significant change of role: instead of having things done to, for and with him, he would himself contribute his time, energy and skills for the benefit of others thus making him feel needed and wanted. Also having the opportunity to make restitution would relieve the burden of rejection and guilt felt by many young offenders while assuaging at the same time feelings of anger and revenge on the community's part.

The Assessment of Needs

To assess children's needs without the availability of the resources necessary to meet them is frustrating to all concerned. Conversely, to allocate children and young people to existing facilities simply because they exist is also unlikely to meet their needs except in a rather hit-or-miss fashion. Faced with this choice of evils, it seems nevertheless wiser to assess the needs of each individual because the findings can be used as ammunition to argue the case for developing those facilities and methods which are lacking. To allocate haphazardly not only reduces the chance of successfully meeting an individual's needs but also risks bringing the whole concept of intermediate treatment into disrepute.

But where, it will be asked, are the resources to come from for developing new facilities and programmes. Taking as a starting point the argument that at a time of financial stringency it is all the more important to make the most effective use of existing resources, should there not be a re-evaluation of those which are most costly, namely residential provision? In a circular issued by the Department of Health and Social Security at the beginning of this year, the case for doing so was persuasively argued. 'A modest switch of resources from residential to intermediate treatment would represent a very substantial increase in resources for intermediate treatment. Any new initiatives in the development of intermediate treatment, involving very little capital expenditure in many cases, would be an investment for the future . . . A successful intermediate treatment programme should considerably reduce the need for residential care providing in many cases a more suitable form of treatment at potentially less cost' (DHSS Circular LAC (77)1).

Where and by whom should the assessment of children and young people be carried out? The answer to this question reflects the continuing unwillingness to pool existing resources belonging to different services. It is now widely accepted that it is comparatively rare to find a single unfavourable or handicapping condition; the more usual picture is a cluster of inter-related and interacting adverse factors. Thus the incidence of educational backwardness is high among children growing up in socioeconomic disadvantage; those who are emotionally deprived and rejected — and they can be found in any home irrespective of social and financial circumstances

— show a high degree of behaviour and learning difficulties; and among young delinquents a significant proportion suffer from both physical and scholastic disabilities.

Hence the assessment procedures required have a broad common base whatever a child's problems. Systematic information is needed about his home circumstances, his health and behavioural history, his current difficulties, his behaviour and attainments in school, and his general personal, social and psychological development. This means that an up-to-date home enquiry and school report must be obtained; and a medical, psychological and educational assessment must be undertaken. Hence, the personnel involved in the diagnostic process are also broadly similar, the basic team consisting of a doctor, educationist, psychologist and social worker. Yet depending on the accident of referral, assessment will be carried out by the school psychological service or the child guidance clinic or a psychiatric hospital unit or an assessment centre, which are respectively under the education or social services department of the local authority or part of the health service.

Surely pooling these different resources would be a more effective use of scarce and expensively specialist manpower? It might also avoid the repeated assessment of the same individuals. In addition, it might contribute towards abolishing the present rather misleading labelling of those referred and help towards developing a better diagnostic system. Centres which integrate all available resources could cater for the whole range of assessments: from the most limited collection and collation of school and home enquiry reports to the other extreme where a prolonged period of skilled observation and examination is essential. In a limited number of cases, this may have to be on a residential rather than a day basis. The aim of all assessment must be the determination of the most appropriate method of intervention and the choice of the most suitable programme of activity to meet ascertained individual needs.

Whither Intermediate Treatment?

A crossroad may well have been reached. Given a real commitment to the concept; adequate resources; staff willing to become involved with a wide range of other professions; youth and community workers able to provide for the differing needs of young people and their families within the community in which they live; and a real partnership between statutory services, voluntary agencies and volunteers; then, and only then, can intermediate treatment really get off the ground to become an imaginative and viable alternative to custodial care.

Most schemes and projects are still in an early stage of development. Monitoring and ongoing evaluation would help to clarify the more effective approaches and methods, as well as providing participating staff with the stimulation and critical awareness which collaboration with practice-orientated researches can — at its best — provide.

If the necessary resources, support and impetus remain lacking and if the belief in the potential efficacy of this approach remains halfhearted, then intermediate treatment may come to share the fate of other innovative and forward looking ideas: to be condemned as ineffective, not because of any inherent shortcomings but because of a failure of imagination and nerve.

References

1 *Children in Trouble* (1968), Cmnd 3601, HMSO.
2 *Children and Young Persons Act* (1969), HMSO.
3 PERSONAL SOCIAL SERVICES COUNCIL (1977), *A Future for Intermediate Treatment*, Report of a study group, PSSC.
4 LEISSNER, A., POWLEY, T. and EVANS, D. (1977), *Intermediate Treatment: A Community-based Action-research Study*, National Children's Bureau.

Chapter 16

Towards a Caring Society?*

Having chosen to leave the Bureau when it comes of age, I shall in my final contribution as Director look back as well as forward. Re-reading the very first article I wrote for the Bureau in 1963, I realized that many of the ideas discussed seem not to have lost their relevance as much as I would have expected in the very different climate of today. Some quotations will illustrate this.

'There is a tendency nowadays to be rather scornful about those early reformers who believed that making provision for improved social welfare would bring about a corresponding decrease in social ills. That high material standards will not abolish them is strongly suggested by the high incidence of violent juvenile crime and the high consumption of tranquillizers in the most affluent of modern societies, the United States.' In fact, in the intervening years these two problems have become endemic also in this country. Additionally drug-abuse and glue-sniffing are now serious health hazards for the young; while rioting has become a new problem in this country. Thus there is probably even greater concern today about children's behaviour than there was eighteen years ago. Meanwhile disenchantment with 'social engineering' — whether by the education, health or social services — has grown apace.

Concluding my thoughts in 1963 about the Bureau's future task, I argued that the far reaching scientific and economic changes which had taken place in the past fifty years made 'considerable demands on the adaptive powers of adults; they also tend to produce anxieties, since all change implies some threat to security. Yet if the challenge of this technological and social revolution is to be met successfully, deeper individual security is needed. On the one hand, it is no longer possible to bring up children with a clear idea or image of the kind of world they will have to

*First published in *Concern*, 41, 1981, pp. 6–15 — the last paper Mia wrote for the Bureau's journal.

live in — few people would hazard a prediction regarding life even twenty or thirty years hence. Yet this makes it all the more important to enable children to grow up emotionally secure as well as adaptable.' Seen in this perspective, the verdict must be that as a society we have so far failed in this task — mainly, I believe, because we have not even started to address ourselves to it.

There have, of course, been improvements during the past eighteen years to which, I think it is fair to claim, the Bureau has made some contribution. What then are these changes for the better?

The Optimism and the Failure of the 'Affluent' Generation

There has been much analysis about the consequences of the 1939–45 war but largely in terms of military, technological and economic consequences. Yet there seems to have been little systematic examination of its emotional and social effects on the generation born in the decade between 1938 and 1948. The vast majority of them grew up in a time of great anxiety, insecurity, change and danger: they were reared in what were virtually one-parent families, since fathers were in the forces, often posted abroad; many mothers worked outside the home to help the war-effort so that their young children were placed in day-nurseries for very long hours; then the return of fathers meant a further period of change and readjustment for all members of the family.

Now these 'war-scarred' children are parents themselves, their children's ages ranging from infancy to the late twenties. May not their disturbed and disrupted childhood experiences account — at least to some extent — for the higher proportion of couples who are now unable to provide secure and consistent care for their own children? Are the rates of high divorce, alcoholism, crime and violence linked to the fact that as adults they have been seeking some compensation for the deprivation of their own childhood? Of course, other factors have contributed, such as changing moral and religious values, more relaxed sexual standards and easier divorce laws.

The aftermath of the war also ushered in a period of great optimism as well as materialism, creating what some have dubbed the 'me' generation. It witnessed steadily increasing affluence for the vast majority; better educational opportunities for both sexes; the rise of the welfare state; and, though poverty was not abolished, it has become far less harsh and crippling; so much so that a TV set and a fridge are now considered almost necessities while obesity is a greater problem among children than malnutrition.

During those years a social and economic revolution took place: rising material standards and full employment led to the euphoria of constantly increasing expectations summed up in the now dated phrase 'you've never had it so good'. This optimistic materialism included wanting 'the best' for one's children. However, this was seen largely in terms of improved health and educational care as well as material aspects such as a room of one's own, more toys, more pocket money and so on.

The failure of this period is that we have not even started to ask the question of how to provide greater emotional security for all children so that they grow up into more caring and more adaptable adults. If anything, the situation may have grown worse as a result of the denigration of the importance of child rearing and caring in general.

Positive Changes

These changes are primarily in attitudes towards and services for the under-fives, children with disabilities, young delinquents and those whose own families cannot care for them. A fifth change — the most recent— concerns the needs and rights of all children and young people.

The Under-Fives

This group began to receive increasing attention during the 1960s and 1970s. Parental self-help and pressure groups, such as the Preschool Playgroups Association and the National Association for the Welfare of Children in Hospital, succeeded in bringing about major changes in practice. Also, while the number of day nursery places declined, both provision for 'rising fives' in infant schools and places in nursery schools increased. However, a large, unmet demand for adequate and high-quality services for this age group remained.

Moreover, existing provision is fragmented, socially divisive and para-doxical. Its fragmentation is reflected in the fact that where the aim is either to complement or to supplement parental care, then it is provided by teachers in educational settings. Where the need is to compensate or sub-stitute for insufficiency or inadequacy of parental care, then it takes place in day nurseries which are staffed by nursery nurses, themselves young, immature and with a much shorter training than teachers. Services are divisive because a much higher proportion of children from middle-class homes go to nursery schools and classes, while the day nurseries and childminders are used mainly by working class parents. It is paradoxical because a charge is made for the latter but not for the former. Now that most secondary schools are comprehensive and primary schools have been so for a long time, it is puzzling why preschool provision remains so rigidly stratified.

The ideal solution would be for all types of preschool provision to be available free of charge, according to the child's needs and parental wishes. For economic reasons this is unlikely to come about for the time being. Would it then not be fairer to make services free for those in need, and then charge the others according to parental ability to pay? Though the means test has always been disliked, is this attitude not an anachronism? After all, everyone has to reveal their income for tax purposes and the parental contribution made for university students also depends on declared family income.

There seems to be no theoretical or practical justification for perpetuating the artificial distinction between pre-school care and education. Many advantages would flow from setting up integrated, multi-purpose, pre-school centres on a neighbourhood basis to provide both care and education in a flexible way.

Children with Disabilities

From the earlier recognition that specific handicaps may require specialized expertise, there developed the view that this need not always mean segregation in special schools. Instead, integration into ordinary schools should be attempted while at the same time making the necessary provision for whatever specific teaching, aids and so on, was required. Also categorizing children according to their major disability was seen to be harmful.

Most important of all, parental involvement in the education and care of their handicapped child began to be seen as crucial in enabling it to overcome, or at least cope optimally with, disabilities. These ideas were put forward in 1970 by a Bureau working party under the chairmanship of the late Dame Eileen Younghusband in the report *Living with Handicap*. Meanwhile the growth of parental self-help movements were making an ever-increasing impact on attitudes as well as on services.

Also our literature reviews of the whole range of childhood disabilities, together with various research projects, all demonstrated the need for rethinking the education and care of children with handicaps; while *Help Starts Here* aimed to enable parents to find their way through the complex maze of organizations and services designed to meet the needs of handicapped children and their families. The Warnock Report incorporated many of these findings and proposals so that they are now to be enshrined in new legislation.

Social Disadvantage and Delinquency

Development during the past eighteen years has been rather paradoxical. On the one hand, children living in severe social disadvantage have been brought to the attention of the public by new pressure groups (such as CPAG and the Council for One-Parent Families); and the Bureau has documented the severity of this problem through its longitudinal National Child Development Study. On the other hand, adequate support for families living in severe disadvantage and services to parents to eradicate the basic causes have been sadly conspicuous by their absence.

In relation to juvenile delinquency the picture is also mixed. The 1969 Act was a forward looking piece of legislation; yet more children and young people find themselves now in custodial establishments, including prisons. The Act fostered a new concept, intermediate treatment, that is, the development of a range of provisions to enable delinquent children, or those at risk of becoming delinquent, to remain in their homes and communities. Also lip service was paid to the desirability of parental involvement, though this has remained fairly rudimentary.

The Bureau's contribution in this field has been a series of linked studies on family advice services, community-based and community-run facilities for young people and their families, and some work on intermediate treatment itself.

Children in Public Care

In the 1950s the emphasis was on reducing the size of children's homes and changing their organization so that, for example, children of different ages and those from the same family could be together. The late 1960s saw a slow acceptance of the view that even improved institutions are not a good place for children to grow up in. Hence renewed interest developed into long-term fostering and into the adoption of so-called 'hard to place children' as well as of those who remained far too long in residential settings in the vain hope that some day their families would be able and willing to accept their care.

Again, the Bureau's review of the literature on substitute care, both in this country and abroad, together with research projects on these topics, helped to bring about these changes. Then the successful establishment of voluntary organizations concentrating on the needs of such children (what is now The British Agencies for Adoption and Fostering as well as the Foster Care Association) was able to bring specialized resources to bear on the further development and practical implementation of these ideas.

Children's Needs and Rights

This is the broadest area of concern. Children's needs are closely linked with increasing knowledge about child development to which the Bureau has made a significant contribution through its 'National Child Development Study'. This was gratifyingly recognised in a book, produced in 1981 by the World Health Organization; surveying some 65 longitudinal studies in Europe, it judged the Bureau's project to be among the three best conducted and most fruitful.

Knowledge about child development is useful only to the extent to which it is actually applied. Hence the recent upsurge of interest in preparation and support for parenthood has been much welcomed by the Bureau and has enabled us to launch a series of initiatives, still underway.

The issue of children's rights has only recently entered public debate and much misunderstanding, even ridicule, surrounds it. Basically it rests on a simple question: why are children denied fundamental, human rights which are assumed almost automatically to be the prerogatives of adults? Or, to put it positively, ought we not to accord children the right to state their point of view; to have some say in decisions which fundamentally affect their future life; and above all, to have the same protection as adults against assault and violence?

So far many of 'The Rights of the Child' in the UN declaration remain unimplemented even in so-called advanced western societies. Now the debate has at least been opened up and the Bureau has made a contribution through its *Who Cares?* project. This gave the opportunity to young people in long-term residential care to make their views known. Though this group is among the most deprived in our society, nevertheless their insights, fairness and often maturity were a surprise even to the most optimistic.

In summary, then, the past two decades have seen improvements in three broad areas. First, the acceptance of the principle, supported by research, that parental involvement is vital to a child's progress and to the effectiveness of services which society provides. Secondly, the understanding, again supported by research, that institutions by their very nature cannot provide truly nurturing environments for human beings, young or old; and, as a corollary, that care, or substitute care, in a family or community setting should be developed wherever possible, even for those severely disabled and emotionally damaged. The third area concerns children's needs and rights where the premise that these should be more widely recognized and met is now being opened up for discussion.

Looking to the Future

That services for children and their families should be improved and in some cases rethought, backed by adequate research, goes without saying. However, neither are in my view, sufficient unless three major changes are brought about in both public and professional attitudes. To do so requires a sustained, imaginative and wide-ranging educational campaign so that these issues are openly faced and widely debated. They are: the image and status of parenthood; the image and status of children; and the relationship between parents and professionals.

I do not have in mind the usual pressure group — although it may well be that this is also needed to monitor closely how social, economic, legislative and other changes affect the interests of children. Whether such a pressure group could be linked with, or contained within, the Bureau is a question which will no doubt be looked at by my successor.

The Image and Status of Parenthood

Recent years have witnessed a devaluing of parenting, and in particular mothering and homemaking. It is difficult to judge how widespread it is since those denigrating it are articulate, vocal and adept at making use of the media. The view propagated is that parenting and homemaking can quite adequately, indeed satisfactorily, be undertaken in the little time left to partners, both of whom have full-time jobs. Hand in hand with this assertion goes the claim that many, if not most women, find caring for young children demoralizing and frustrating as well as damaging to their self-image because, so it is argued, under-fives are boring, irksome and demanding whereas paid jobs outside the home are rewarding, challenging and interesting. To my mind, this is a disingenuous, if not dishonest, portrayal of the working conditions of the vast majority.

Many young people are disenchanted with contemporary society which, after all, has been largely made by men: it values self-assertion, competition and status-seeking rather than compassion, conciliation and sensitivity to the needs of others. Though this world has achieved much to be proud of in terms of scientific and technological achievements, it is in the sphere of relationships between individuals as well as relations between different nations that only limited progress has been made.

In seeking a more creative and happier mode of living, so-called feminine characteristics and values will have to come to the fore, both in public and private life. A greater emphasis on the quality of life may perhaps begin to blur the dividing line between the male and female worlds. Feminine values are quite essential not only for the mere survival of the human race but equally for the quality of compassion and care which our society should be willing to extend to all its members. Children are the seed corn for the future: it is the loved and cared-for child who is enabled to become eventually a caring adult and loving parent. At present the needs of the handicapped and the old are much emphasized, yet their needs will be poorly served in times to come, if children are reared by parents whose role and contribution to the common good are denigrated and devalued.

The educational campaign referred to earlier would have to tackle two major obstacles. The first is the male-orientated labour market which finds it more convenient to take a traditional view of women's place in and contribution to the workforce. Surely there are no insuperable difficulties in enabling mothers (or fathers if a couple so wishes to arrange its family life) to devote four to ten years out of a potential working lifespan of forty or more years to creating appropriate flexible working conditions for those rearing young children?

The second major obstacle is economic. Today the relative financial position of parents compared with non-parents is worse than it was forty years ago. This deterioration is due in part to the tax and welfare policies of successive governments, and in part to the increasing costs of caring for children. Fragmentation characterizes the present system of family income support, and insufficient recognition is being given to the serious financial pressures facing families with dependent children. Nor is sufficient attention paid to the link between these pressures (which include poor housing, chronic ill-health and unemployment) and the incidence, if not increase, in vandalism, truancy, delinquency and educational failure. Compared with the other EEC countries, Britain lags considerably behind in providing family income support.

As the Outer Circle Policy Unit has argued, generous but taxable child benefits phased into a system of tax relief could prevent hardship, greatly reduce relative deprivation and, provided they were part of a coordinated tax and welfare system, would encourage parental responsibility and self-reliance. Family income support does not come cheap but its long-term benefits are incalculable. Children are after all the wealth creators of tomorrow upon whose efforts and abilities all our futures depend. So the question is not whether we can afford to but rather whether we can afford not to give such support to families.

Changing Attitudes towards Children

Just as parenting, and mothering in particular, is glamourized in the abstract and devalued in practice, so are attitudes to children. On the one hand there is a warmhearted, often sentimental, portrayal of children in the abstract together with compassionate sympathy with their suffering (for example starving children abroad, or child murderers having to be protected in prisons from their fellow inmates). On the other hand, far too many adults — both parents and professionals — behave towards children in a way totally different to that adopted towards other adults.

Examples abound and can be observed daily in streets, supermarkets, classrooms and hospitals. Why do so many adults feel justified in depriving children of the courtesy and consideration which they extend to adult human beings? The tone of voice used; the criticisms levelled, both in private and public, about a child's looks, abilities and appearance; the dislike shown to children in shops, on transport and in hotels; all these and more are a reflection of the double standards prevalent in practice among people who would claim to be concerned for children.

In courts of law there is an even more curious double standard in cases of child murder. If the adult kills a child which is not his own, then he is likely to receive a severe sentence; but when a parent commits the same act, the penalty is much lighter and often derisory. The fact that the child may have screamed or had 'dirty habits' are considered ameliorating circumstances, as if a baby can reasonably be blamed for 'provoking' violence in the same way as a drunken husband or a nagging wife. Indeed, even the term 'murder' is avoided in cases where a child has been killed by his parent.

I am not, of course, questioning that there are many laws designed to protect the interests of children and that at times these may even ride roughshod over the rights of parents. Nor do I deny that children can be tiresome, difficult, aggressive and a nuisance. But this is part of being an immature human being. And surely this does not justify viewing all children as if they are potential wrongdoers? After all, we do not treat most adults as potential liars, thieves or murderers even though some of them are just that.

A final (and perhaps most telling) example is the attitude towards corporal punishment. It is so much part of childrearing that even the majority of young children are regularly hit by their parents. Similarly, teachers can use the cane on five year olds as well as on children who are physically or mentally handicapped. The belief in the usefulness of corporal punishment is curious, when there is no evidence to support it. On the contrary, several studies show that children are better behaved in schools where it is not used; and since all too often the same pupils are punished in this way, it is clearly ineffective in changing behaviour.

For some years now, physical punishment has been abolished by law in the armed forces, in prisons, borstals and detention centres. So is it not illogical as well as unjust, to continue to inflict corporal punishment on children? Is it not hypocritical to condemn their aggressive behaviour when we practise it on them as a matter of course; and disingenuous when we profess to set children a good example of how to behave by the way we ourselves do? Physical chastisement may even be counterproductive since it not only arouses aggression but, equally important, teaches an unintended but none the less obvious lesson: that 'might is right' and hence if you are bigger you can intimidate and hit those weaker than yourself.

Our society no longer believes in the ennobling effects of pain — instead people consume a vast array of medicines and drugs to escape discomfort and alleviate pain. Why then do we continue to cling to the belief that deliberately inflicted pain on the young is educative and morally reforming?

Can all these seemingly perverse attitudes be explained by the fact that as adults most of us have forgotten what it feels like to be a child? Are we conditioned by society, and may be also due to some instinctive reactions, to feel kindly towards the young yet many people do not really enjoy close contact with them? In my view, discrimination against children is widespread, pervasive and harmful in its long-term effects as sex or racial discrimination. Because it is so generally connived at, its eradication is bound to be a very slow process, even if the will is created to achieve it. To create this will in all sections of society is a task of major importance. If the seed corn of society is allowed to rot — even if only in part — the price exacted cannot be compensated for in economic growth and technological advancement.

Relations Between Parents and Professionals

The rise of professionalism in the field of child development has — inadvertently — underminded the confidence of many parents in their own ability to cope. The fact that the different professional workers do not speak with one voice and may even give conflicting advice, has further contributed to parental uncertainty, as has the general climate of fading faith in religious and moral imperatives. In a world as uncertain not only where it is going but where it wants or ought to go, the bringing up of children has become an ever more difficult task.

Professional workers all too often underestimate parental knowledge and insight — a failing shared by many a doctor, psychologist, teacher, social worker and therapist. Inevitably this is communicated to parents when they are seeking advice and help; in turn, it will contribute to their inability to give a fully adequate account of the reasons for their concern. Also people tend to be somewhat in awe of professional experts. In unfamiliar surroundings many are liable to have difficulty in marshalling their thoughts; and special interviews and examinations are likely to engender stress and anxiety, which then make one appear less competent. These reactions in turn serve to confirm the professional workers' attitudes, leading them to underestimate parental understanding even further. So both sides are liable to become locked in a mutually reinforcing circle of mis-apprehension, to the detriment of the child's well-being.

If parents are to be accepted as full partners, then the role as well as the attitude of the 'expert' must change. She or he must translate into practical recognition the fact that it is parents who play by far the most important part in the care, health and education of their children, particularly during the vital early years; that most are deeply concerned for their well-being and development; but because childrearing is a complex and challenging task, many parents become anxious at times about the significance of a problem and doubt whether their handling of it is appropriate. Consequently parental anxiety must be taken seriously, even if it is a reflection of inexperience, self-doubt or exhaustion. A willingness to listen, to offer reassurance and guidance may be all that is required.

Parents are potentially the best 'detectors' of handicap. More attention should be paid to that rather maligned sixth sense 'maternal instinct', because it is often the mother who has the first suspicion that all is not well with her child. To be told either 'not to worry' or that the child will 'grow out of it' is a disservice, since such advice is unlikely to allay her anxiety which itself may have an adverse effect on the child's emotional development.

At times, the worries expressed may not be directly related to the child but due to the mother missing the daily companionship of adults at work; to loneliness when having moved to a new area; to unsuitable housing conditions or to marital difficulties. Then the professional task is to give reassurance about the normality of the child's development and helping the mother to recognize the underlying problem and consider possible remedies.

Secondly, the self-help movements may well signal a return to community care. The latter has become a very fashionable but vague slogan. In fact the community, or more concretely, women in the community have always shouldered the main burden of caring: for children, the handi-capped, the sick and old. Hitherto they have been taken for granted, being expected to do this while often sacrificing their chance of marriage or a career; and without proper financial recompense or adequate support. Moreover the burden of low income, bad housing and insufficient food always bears heaviest on women who put the needs of dependents, especially their children, before their own.

By generating self-help movements, by mobilizing young people as volunteers and, in future, by harnessing to a greater extent the energies of the retired, redundant and unemployed, a renewed sense of mutual involvement in the welfare of one's neighbourhood could be created. It must include giving practical help of all kinds to caregiving women so as to lighten their load of unremitting responsibility for immature, aged or infirm dependents. In this way, a true spirit of community care can be fostered, rooted in and springing from individuals who value self-reliance, practical action and a measure of independence from authority and from professional expertise. In the process many will discover or rediscover that the 'gift relationship' enriches not only the recipient but also the giver. Children growing up in such a mutually supportive environment are likely, in turn, to grow into adults willing to invest in caring.

Can Such Changes in Attitudes Be Achieved?

There are many voices ready to dismiss the possibility on the grounds of original sin; or the complexity of the human personality; or the belief that the urge to compete is stronger than the wish to cooperate; to name just a few of the arguments brought to bear. But surely failure should not be assumed unless we first attempt to bring about such changes with a whole-hearted commitment and belief in their viability?

This is not a hopeless task but it is one that can seem infinitely long. The record of human progress is replete with examples of the ways in which the consistent advocacy of humane objectives has moulded public attitudes and political policies. It is from our past progress that I draw my present optimism. Our current concerns about the mentally sick, the handicapped and the lawbreakers, about environmental pollution and the effects of smoking, stand in a great tradition that has brought about social change in the past. It is not too much to hope that what I and the Bureau have advocated will, in time, come about. A truly caring society has been the age-old dream of man. I believe this must have its foundations in that fairer future for all our children for which we have worked. I know that the Bureau, under my successor, will continue to contribute to this end. And that it will contribute most significantly.

References

MEDNICK, S.A. and BAERT, A.E. (Ed) (1981) *Perspective Longitudinal Research*, Oxford University Press for WHO.
PARKER, H. (1978) *Who Pays for the Children?* The Outer Circle Policy Unit, London.
PRINGLE, M.K. (1980) *A Fairer Future for Children*, Macmillan.

Chapter 17

A Policy For Families — Or For Children?*

It is fashionable at present to dispute that a policy for children is required and to stress instead the need for a family policy. This view rests on the belief that what is good for the family must be good for children. For the majority, this is probably true. However, the extent to which this is so has not yet been explored, nor have we looked at the areas of conflict between the interests of parents and their offspring.

To my mind, it is preferable to frame a policy which places the major emphasis on the needs of children. First, because of hostility to government intervention; second, because of conflicting interests of adults and children; and third, because today's children will be tomorrow's citizens.

Hostility to Government Intervention

In democratic societies at least, there is resistance to, and indeed suspicion of, state interference in people's private lives. Adults are considered to be responsible for the way in which they conduct their personal affairs; and they can only be deprived of the liberty to do so in very specific, legally defined ways. This is so even when a man's behaviour is blatantly irresponsible, such as gambling away most of his earnings, to the detriment of his family's welfare.

It is arguable to what extent adults should be protected, either by legislation or by heavier taxation, against harming themselves, for example by drink or tobacco.

For children, however, the position is different. When parents or those *in loco parentis* fail to exercise their responsibilities adequately, then surely as

*First published in *Concern*, 22, 1976–77, pp. 25–29.

the agent of society, government must intervene to ensure that their well-being is safeguarded. Of course, education and persuasion should be used first. But what if these fail? That the issues are complex and delicate is beyond doubt nor are there any simple answers. But in arguing for a policy for children, the question of the children's liberty assumes to my mind a different dimension.

Conflicting Interests of Adults and Children

Children are totally dependent upon adults. They have no independent voice, no vote and few rights in law. In fact, most laws are in the nature of directions and prohibitions, limiting their choices although many are, of course, designed to protect their health and welfare. Adults, for example, can choose their place of work and have some influence on their working conditions. In contrast, children are forced to go to school, even when they are patently unhappy and failing to derive much benefit from their education; also they have no influence on the choice of school or class which they must attend.

This example also illustrates the fact that the interest of the parent does not necessarily coincide with that of the child. On the one hand, compulsory school attendance frees the mother from her responsibility for full-time care. Thus, it provides her with much more free time for her own interests, including paid employment. On the other hand, many five-year-olds are not ready for full-time education, either physcially, emotionally, socially or intellectually, and in some cases, on all four grounds. For them, part-time education or even postponing it until they are more mature would be an advantage. In fact, Britain and a few of the Commonwealth countries are alone in the world in making full-time schooling compulsory from such an early age (that is, from 9 am to 4 pm).

Another area of potential conflict between the interests of the child and his parents is family size. On the one hand, the idea of a large family appeals to many couples; moreover, some women feel happiest and healthiest during pregnancy and the early months of their baby's life. On the other hand, research shows that children develop less well if they grow up in a large, rather than a small, family. A family-centred policy would regard the number of children a couple choose to have as a private matter; and child benefits would be paid regardless of how many there are.

In contrast, a policy concerned with the best interests of children would make widely known the effects of family size on children. Educational means might be used to change attitudes. Family planning services would be made available on a priority basis to those who already have two children. And government would choose to design child benefit and tax allowances in such a way as to give the greatest financial support for the first and second child while tailing off allowances steeply for subsequent children.

Uneconomic Priorities and Fragmented Services

The lack of a coherent policy for children is probably the chief reason why we continue to accept irrational priorities and remain prepared to pay the most for the least effective provision. A few examples will illustrate this.

Though family allowances will be paid for the first-born child from 1977 onwards, it will be at a lower rate than for subsequent children. Yet the arrival of the first child causes the most marked drop in parental income. Until then, the vast majority of women will have been going out to work. Subsequently only a tiny minority (some six per cent) return to full-time work before the child starts school. In addition, for the first baby, everything has to be bought, from the pram and clothes to furniture and toys.

In the educational field, the average size of class becomes smaller the older the pupils. Yet the older they are the more they can learn by themselves under the teacher's guidance. In contrast, while children acquire the basic skills during the primary school stage, a great deal of individual attention is essential. With classes of 35 or more, this is patently impossible. In consequence, more costly remedial work and literacy programmes have to be provided for secondary school pupils and for adults.

In the field of child care, evidence is now incontestable that life in institutions has damaging effects on many of the inmates, be they hospital patients, borstal boys or children. Yet this most costly form of care continues to be used for ever-increasing numbers. Some £110 million is spent on residential care, while only about £14 million is invested in day care. In other countries (Sweden, for example), the position is reversed.

In the medical field, play in hospital is a simple example. The opportunity to play enables children to cope better with the inevitable separation from home, the fear, the pain as well as the effects of surgical and other procedures. The cost of a play leader is relatively cheap compared with the total cost of a hospital stay. Yet a significant proportion of hospitals fail to provide one.

A last example comes from the planning field. In cities, more space is allocated to car parks than to children's play facilities. Consequently, over 1000 are killed each year (three daily) and 15,000 seriously injured. Even ignoring the pain, grief and loss of life, the cost of providing long-term treatment, if not lifelong care, for the worst affected is extremely high.

Irrational priorities are uneconomic in human as well as in financial terms. Failure to provide adequate support and preventive services for all children means that later on much more expensive rehabilitation, treatment or punitive facilities have to be paid for.

Three Guiding Principles for a Policy for Children

The first principle is a national commitment to the well-being of children, especially the youngest age-group. At a time when resources are limited, is there not a case for concentrating them where they can do the most good? Economic constraints could even be turned to advantage if they led to a more effective use of available knowledge and resources. If paramountcy were to be accorded to the child's best interests, then it will affect the setting of priorities in many areas; central and local government policy as well as industry and commerce will be faced with rather different criteria. For example, how to make cities as suitable environments for children as for adults and their cars; whether to give more support to family care than to substitute group day care; how to make working hours more flexible to enable both men and women to devote more time to their families; how to enable couples wishing to share a paid job and child-rearing to do so.

The second principle follows from the first; namely to accept parents as full partners with the professionals who plan and staff the services provided for children. If responsible parenthood is to be encouraged, then parental involvement must not only be welcomed but fostered. Perhaps the most glaring example of their current exclusion is seen in the education system: how children are taught, what they are expected to learn; whether or not they are subjected to physical chastisement; whether or not they are ready for full-time schooling at the age of five years; in relation to none of these issues are parents' wishes either ascertained or taken into account.

The third principle lies in the recognition that no single department of local or central government, and no single profession has 'the key' either to promoting children's all-round development or to providing solutions to disadvantage and deprivation. The key will only be found through inter-departmental, interdisciplinary cooperation. Hence, the pooling of knowledge, of skills and of resources is an essential prerequisite.

Community resources — voluntary workers, self-help organizations and the whole range of voluntary bodies— must be included. Professional training clearly plays a central part in laying the basis for such a collabor-ative philosophy and practice. So is the acceptance that working for and with children demands specific knowledge and skills, which fully justify specialization.

That problems of incredible complexity *can* be solved has been shown by the spectacular success of space exploration, accomplished in a relatively short period of time. The key, as I see it, was a vast commitment of resources to an equally vast collaborative exercise between scientists and practitioners from a wide spectrum of disciplines. Are there not lessons to be learned from this achievement about merging all the relevant professional interests in a commitment to the well-being of children?

Setting new Priorities

Translating these three principles into practice means that planning, and the selection of priorities in particular, must go 'across the board', including social, health, education and environmental services (such as housing and employment). Corporate planning has now become an accepted principle at local government level, if not yet a fully worked out procedure. A beginning has been made too with setting up joint planning teams and with establishing joint financing arrangements.

There is a strong case for creating further joint planning teams. Perhaps the most suitable areas to begin with are assessment services, provision for the under-fives and intermediate treatment facilities, all of which already involve participation by more than one profession and department. Family planning and preparation for parenthood are two other areas with great potential for joint planning and cooperation at fieldwork level.

Much greater flexibility in the allocation of funds and in the use of other resources would be advantageous. For example, viring from education should be considered in order to redress the present neglect of the under-fives and of disadvantaged youngsters, when compared with spending on sixth-formers and university students. Similarly, operational coordination across not only departmental but agency boundaries could facilitate a fuller use of existing facilities.

Examples are the use of nursery schools by those attending day nurseries; the use of playgroups by childminders; of sports facilities belonging to schools by intermediate treatment projects; of community homes for training mothers in child care, and so on.

In deciding on the best use of existing resources, it is also necessary to choose between putting up more residential buildings and training more staff. Surely the latter would be a better investment? Both take a matter of years to provide, but people are a more flexible resource than bricks and mortar. The acceptance of this fact has been slow in coming. For example, it has been decided — even in this time of severe economic restraint — to build more secure units for delinquents despite all the evidence on the ineffectiveness of closed institutions to 'reform' them.

Once the areas for redistribution of funds and resources have been indentified, it would, of course, be up to the local authorities and local planning groups to choose the options most suited to local needs. This may involve grants from central to local government becoming more flexible. Also, services vary widely from one part of the country to another in both quality and quantity. Might it help to raise standards if central government were to issue guidelines about desirable minimum standards, at least for those services where the local authority stands *in loco parentis*?

Lastly, young people should be helped to achieve a more realistic understanding of parenthood long before becoming parents. This may lead some couples to question whether they are really willing to devote the necessary time, energy and money to caring for children; and if not, to decide against raising a family. For the majority, however, raising children is the most creative and responsible task likely to be available to them. The fact that today most mothers even of secondary age children, choose not to work full-time (only 18 per cent do so) bears witness to this.

At present, only a minority of school-leavers have sufficient opportunity to learn about psychological aspects of family life and about the care of babies. The results of our recently published national study of 16-year-olds showed that two-thirds had no chance to do so in school. Significantly enough, the young people themselves were aware of their need to know more — nearly 60 percent of them would have liked to learn more about these aspects of adult responsibility.

The vast majority of schools taught the physical aspects of human reproduction (90 per cent in our national study just referred to). But surely it is paradoxical, if not irresponsible, to provide sex education without matching this with information on contraception; and, even more important, with a consideration of the emotional and personal aspects of sexual relationships? Yet this was done in far fewer schools (55 per cent and 67 per cent respectively).

In my view, encouraging responsible and informed parenthood is an integral part of a policy for children. Then the parental life-style may come to be chosen more deliberately, in the full realisation of its demands, constraints, satisfactions and challenges. Changing the image of homemaking and childrearing should be part of this realization. Otherwise there is a danger that children become pawns in the quest for economic prosperity and in the battle for women's liberation. The risks in allowing this to happen are great — both in terms of their happiness and society's future.

Chapter 18

Putting Children First*

The past thirty years have seen better educational opportunities for both boys and girls; greatly increased affluence for the vast majority; and though poverty and unemployment continue to exist, neither is now as harsh or crippling as in the thirties. A television set and fridge are considered necessities; and obesity is a greater problem among children than malnutrition. Why then the continuing symptoms of social disease and malaise, reflected in the high rate of divorce, of consumption of tranquillisers and other drugs, alcoholism, delinquency, crime and violence? Perhaps the experience of the last war holds a clue.

The Long-Term Effects of the 1939–45 War

Might the years from 1939 to 1945 have had more pervasive and lasting emotional and social effects than has hitherto been realized? Since it was the first time that the whole civilian population, including children, was affected, this is perhaps a plausible assumption. Those born in the decade between 1937 and 1947 grew up in a time of great anxiety, insecurity, change and danger. With fathers in the forces, many of them posted abroad, most children were reared single-handed by their mothers; moreover as many of them worked outside the home to help the war effort, their young children were placed in day nurseries for long hours; also evacuation separated many children from their own homes. Then the return of fathers to their families and civilian life meant a further period of change and readjustment for all members of the family.

Those born during the decade in question are now between 32 and 42 years of age; by now most of them will be the parents of children aged

*First published in *Concern*, 33, 1979, pp. 5–10.

between 10 and 20 years. Might the disturbed and disrupted childhood experiences of this war-time generation account — at least to some extent — for the increase in broken relationships in their own lives and for a higher proportion of couples who are unable to provide secure and good-enough care for their own children? These in turn are linked to mental illness, crime and violence.

Yet during these disturbed and disturbing war years, the community also determined to 'put children first' in relation to physical safety and physical well-being. Evacuation was one measure, the effect of which has never been properly investigated, even in retrospect. The other was a deliberate policy of positive discrimination regarding diet and health. When food supplies were threatened by blockade, it was realized that starvation could imperil the future of a whole generation. Therefore special provision was made for expectant and nursing mothers and for children. The benefits of this courageous decision are still evident today. A virtual revolution in children's health has taken place, evidenced by their being taller and maturing earlier with malnutrition being largely a memory of the past.

Promoting a Greater Commitment to Children

We are now coming face to face with the consequences of impersonal technological, scientific and industrial progress; of the ever more competitive greed of a consumer society; of the wasteful squandering of our national resources, including human potential; and of the price exacted by the rat-race on our sense of values as well as on our physical and mental health. In what direction should we go to ensure a happier, more creative and fulfilled future for today's children?

Need we find a different commitment — a commitment with a more human face? A socially fairer and juster society means a community which no longer tolerates that amidst general affluence one child in sixteen grows up in squalor and deprivation; and that valuable human potential is destined to remain tragically and wastefully unfulfilled among a sizeable minority of tomorrow's parents (Wedge and Prosser, 1973).

Can such a change in public attitudes be brought about? There are many voices ready to dismiss this possibility. But surely, there can be no certainty of the outcome unless we first attempt to bring about such a change with a wholehearted commitment and belief in its viability. After all, changes in public attitudes have been achieved in other areas, such as more humane views about the mentally sick, the handicapped and law breakers as well as more recently on environmental pollution and smoking.

The Basic Ingredients of Early Care

There can be no doubt by now that a child's psychological development is profoundly and significantly influenced by the kind of care s/he receives. Though development is ultimately limited by biological and genetic factors, it is the quality of care which determines the extent to which all the infant's potentialities will eventually be realized. The essential ingredients of such care are unconditional affection and acceptance; appropriate and varied intellectual stimulation; and responsive interaction.

During the first three years of life, a dependable, consistent, warm, mutually satisfying and continuous relationship is crucial to optimal development. Most mothers find it rewarding to have the time to enjoy, and to be closely involved in, their child's rapid growth which takes place during these vital years. In turn this intimate and absorbing involvement is an important factor which influences the rate and the quality of the infant's progress. Full-time maternal care (or for that matter paternal care) is unique in the sense that it allows the mother time to develop sensitivity to her baby which then enables her to recognize and adapt to his or her very individual needs.

The women's liberation movement justifiably demands equal rights in education, training, employment and career prospects as well as in marriage. By choosing to ignore one vital difference between the sexes, namely that only women can conceive and bear children, the movement has — wittingly or otherwise — brought about a serious devaluing both of mothering and parenthood.

Putting Children First

Surely there are no insuperable difficulties in enabling mothers (or fathers if a couple so wishes to arrange its family life) to devote four to ten years out of a potential working life span of forty or more years to caring for their young children? The only obstacles at present are those created by a largely man-made and male-orientated labour market which finds it easier and more convenient to take a conservative, traditional view of women's place in and contribution to the work force.

Employers and trade unions alike refuse to acknowledge — or, more irresponsibly still, even fail to consider — the needs of young children. They gloss over the fact that high quality day nurseries and crèches are a very expensive provision and reject the evidence that group methods of care for under-threes are not the best way of meeting their needs. Even though paying a child care allowance or greatly increased child benefit would be less costly solutions, trade unions and the women's liberation movement object to them by arguing that they could be used as a means of 'pushing women back into the home'; they also claim that employers would find it easier to dismiss mothers without having a bad social conscience.

Surely the way to reconcile these differences should be to acknowledge that by bringing up a family a mother is performing a social and economic task which is every bit as important as any contribution she might have made, and may again make, to business, industry, commerce or the professions. She (and her husband) should be able to choose how to cope with the dual, and at times competing, demands of paid work outside the home and child care responsibilities; and she should have the opportunity to make this choice free from economic, social or emotional pressures.

It can be done — for example, in Hungary a special child care allowance is paid to mothers for the first three years after a child's birth. Though it is dependent on their not having an outside paid job during that period, the time spent at home does not constitute a break in employment. On her return to work a mother will have her wages or salary adjusted in such a way that she is not penalized financially or promotion-wise because of the period devoted to child rearing. This system has been in force since 1967.

Sharing the Cost of Children

Insufficient recognition is being given to the serious financial pressures facing families with dependent children. Nor is sufficient attention paid to the link between these pressures (which include poor housing and the consequences of chronic ill-health) and the incidence, if not increase, in vandalism, truancy, delinquency and educational failure. Compared with the other EEC countries, Britain lags behind in family income support, welfare politics being dominated by the pensioners' lobby.

A recent report (Parker, 1978) claimed that 'the post-war system of family income support, which from the outset lacked coherence, has been reduced by the events of 33 years to a jungle of contradictions and anomalies which endanger the very foundations of our society, and for which the Child Benefit Act in its present form offers no sure solution . . . We live in a patriarchal society, where the rights of children as equal citizens are studiously ignored.'

The financial burden of raising children should no longer be regarded as largely the duty of parents alone but as a shared responsibility between society and those individuals who are willing to undertake this onerous task.

Of course, monetary support can in no way fully reimburse parents for inevitably long 'hours of duty', asocial hours and a lowered standard of living compared with childless couples. But choices have always to be paid for and there are, of course, many compensating joys and rewards in raising a family for those who truly love children.

Today's Children — Tomorrow's Citizens

By putting the interests and well-being of children first, we would give practical recognition to the fact that they are the seed-corn of the future. Their development determines the fabric of tomorrow's society. Whether it will be more cohesive and more tolerant of racial and cultural differences; whether the incidence of mental stress, violence, vandalism, and crime will increase or diminish; all these depend to a very considerable degree on the priority which we are willing to accord to meeting adequately the needs of growing children today. The ability to care grows from having experienced loving care. In the long run, a policy for children will benefit parents too, though in the shorter term it may limit the degree of their choice and freedom to some extent.

Too often it is judged more urgent or more feasible to consider the relative costs of different policies in terms of tax payers' money rather than the psychological effects, that is, the kind of children or adults we are creating and the kind we want. Instead, it might be helpful to set out those aims or goals of child care policies on which there is probably a broad consensus.

The first is to promote the physical development of children. This involves much more than simple survival and the prevention of handicap; it must be concerned with the quality of life, the promotion of physical vitality and the whole range of motor skills.

The second is to promote the psychological development of children, which covers an even wider range of skills, behaviour and qualities. Among them are language and communication; resourcefulness and coping strategies; intellectual growth and scholastic attainments; and, above all, the capacity for caring and sharing, for developing emotional attachment, warmth, trust and willingness to help others. Perhaps the term which best summarizes the aims of psychological development is 'overall competence' which is reflected in all the child's behaviour — relations with other people, the use and understanding of language, knowledge of social situations and involvement in creative activities.

The third aim is to provide children with a pleasant childhood, free from hunger and pain, insecurity and fear, pressure and stress, abuse and neglect. This aim is seldom made explicit in policy statements — perhaps because it seems obvious or is thought to be too 'unscientific'. It nevertheless deserves mention because it is the hallmark of a civilized society that childhood is treated as an important period for its own sake and not merely as a preparation for adulthood.

The second and third aims are interrelated. Perhaps the puritanical ethic has held sway for too long, on the mistaken assumption that happiness and high standards are incompatible. Commonsense has rather satisfyingly received support from recent research which shows that academic achievement in socially deprived areas is more influenced by the ethos, positive values and encouragement given by the school, and by the personal example and attitudes of the teachers, than by such aspects as the age of the buildings, the size of the school or the amount of punishment (Rutter *et al.* 1979).

Happiness and academic achievements are thus seen not to be alternatives but to go together. If this is so for adolescents, then it is bound to be the case to an even greater extent in the far closer relationships between parents and children: it is neither income, social position nor severity of discipline, but the loving care, personal example and positive encouragement given by parents which promote happy as well as capable children. In short, it is the loved, cared for infant who in turn becomes the loving, caring adult.

Putting children first means that in the framing of policies a number of basic issues must be resolved: how to encourage and support good parenting; when and how to identify children 'at risk' so as to mitigate the effects of handicap or of neglect, deprivation and ill-treatment; how to intervene for the sake of the child's safety and happiness; and how to improve the care of children growing up apart from their biological families.

Grounds for Optimism

There is a tendency in this country to belittle our achievements and to compare ourselves unfavourably with other nations. This attitude leads to the danger of talking ourselves into a mood of unjustified gloom and defeatism. In fact, there are substantial grounds for optimism. For one thing, rather than being 'the sick man of Europe', as both academic economists and the media claim, a careful American analyst comes to the opposite conclusion: 'In the first 30 years after World War II, Britain enjoyed the fastest rate of economic growth in its recorded history . . . This unprecedented growth has transformed the living standards of ordinary people. When the Queen celebrated her Silver Jubilee in 1977, each of her subjects on average enjoyed incomes commanding almost four-fifths more in goods and services than their parents. Even allowing for a great rise in prices, 'real' and not inflated incomes after taxes had grown by 88 per cent between 1952 and 1976' (Nossiter, 1978).

The author goes on to demonstrate that similar improvements were shown by a host of other indicators such as health, infant mortality, the life expectation of men and women, the proportion of people who have an indoor lavatory, a bath, a car and a TV set. Moreover, 'the rising tide of prosperity had lifted the poor as well as the rich. The number living below the poverty line fell from one-fifth of the population in 1953–4 to one-fortieth in 1973, an eightfold gain . . . Britons got richer; their neighbours got richer faster. That is the hard core of fact in the layers of gloom produced in the popular pulpits.'

If Nossiter's analysis is correct — and I for one find it convincing — then surely there are grounds for hoping that just as this country has pioneered the belief that society has a responsibility for its more vulnerable members, so we shall develop an increasing regard for the needs and rights of the most vulnerable yet most promising members of our society — our children.

References

NOSSITER, D.D. (1978) *Britain — A Future that Works*, Andre Deutsch.
PARKER, H. (1978) *Who Pays for the Children?* The Outer Circle Policy Unit.
PRINGLE, M.K. (1980) *A Fairer Future for Children*, Macmillan.
RUTTER, M. *et al* (1979) *Fifteen Thousand Hours: Secondary Schools and their Effects on Children*, Open Books.
WEDGE, P. and PROSSER, H. (1973) *Born to Fail?* Arrow Books for NCB.

Ten Child Care Commandments*

Ten Child Care Commandments

1 Give continuous, consistent, loving care — it's as essential for the mind's health as food is for the body.

2 Give generously of your time and understanding — playing with and reading to your child matters more than a tidy, smooth-running home.

3 Provide new experiences and bathe your child in language from birth onwards — they enrich his growing mind.

4 Encourage him to play in every way both by himself and with other children — exploring, imitating, constructing, pretending and creating.

5 Give more praise for effort than for achievement.

6 Give him ever-increasing responsibility — like all skills, it needs to be practised.

7 Remember that every child is unique — so suitable handling for one may not be right for another.

8 Make the way you show disapproval fit your child's temperament, age and understanding.

9 Never threaten that you will stop loving him or give him away; you may reject his behaviour but never suggest that you might reject him.

10 Don't expect gratitude; your child did not ask to be born — the choice was yours.

*Taken from *The Needs of Children* (Hutchinson, 1974; 2nd ed. 1980; 3rd ed. 1986) — a personal perspective commissioned by the Department of Health and Social Security.

Mia Kellmer Pringle — A Bibliography

1949 'Vocational guidance', in SWINDON J.B. *Careers in Local Government*.
1950 *Intelligence, Social Maturity and Environment*, London, British Association.
      A Study of Doll's Social Maturity Scale as Applied to a Representative Sample of British Children Between the Age of Six and Eight Years, PhD Thesis, London, Birkbeck College.
1951 'Social maturity and social competence. Part 1. Social maturity and its assessment', *Educational Review*, 3, 2, pp. 113–28.
      'Social maturity and social competence. Part 2. A study of Doll's Vineland social maturity scale', *Educational Review*, 3, 2, pp. 183–95.
1952 'Case study and the techniques of individual diagnosis', *Educational Review*, 4, 3, pp. 170–6. (with WALL, W.D.)
      'Problem children', *The Schoolmaster*, 162, 2252–6, pp. 319, 349, 387, 413, 455. (5 articles)
      'The remedial education centre', *National Froebel Foundations Journal*, April, p. 11.
1953 'A note on an evaluation of remedial education', *British Journal of Educational Psychology*, 23, 3, pp. 196–9. (with GULLIFORD, R.)
1954 'Learning difficulties of the deprived child', *Hospital and Social Service Journal*, 5, pp. 27–36.
      'The remedial education centre', *British Journal of Physical Medicine*, 17, pp. 121–8.
1955 'A training college for teachers of the handicapped in Hungary', *Special Schools Journal*, 44, pp. 26–9.
1956 'The backward child', *Times Educational Supplement*, 12, 19 October, 9 November.
1957 'Differences between schools for the maladjusted and ordinary boarding schools', *British Journal of Educational Psychology*, 27, 1, pp. 29–36.
      'The educational needs of deprived children', *Child Care*, 11, 1, pp. 4–8.
      'An experiment in parent-staff group discussion', *Educational Review*, 9, 2, pp. 128–35.
      'A note on the use of the Schonell and Gates reading tests in the first year of the junior school', *British Journal of Educational Psychology*, 27, 2, pp. 135–41. (with NEALE, M.D.)
      'The study of exceptional children', *International Review of Education*, 3, 2, pp. 200–9.

1958 'The department of child study', *University of Birmingham Gazette*, 11, pp. 23–5.
'The effects of early deprivation on speech development: A comparative study of 4 year olds in a nursery school and in residential nurseries', *Language and Speech*, 1, 4, pp. 269–97. (with TANNER, M.)
'Learning and emotion', *Educational Review*, 10, 2, pp. 146–68.
'Reading at home and abroad', *Educational Review*, 11, pp. 68–71.
'Research without tears', *Education for Teaching*, 48, pp. 49–51.
'A study of deprived children. Part 1: Intellectual, emotional and social development', *Vita Humana*, 1, 2, pp. 65–92. (with BOSSIO, V.)
'A study of deprived children. Part 2: Language development and reading attainment', *Vita Humana*, 1, 3–4, pp. 142–70. (with BOSSIO, V.)

1959 'Comparative study of the effects of early deprivation on speech development', *Perceptual and Motor Skills*, 9, pp. 345–6.
'The emotional and social development of deprived children', in *Proceedings of the XVth International Congress of Psychology, Brussels, 1957.* (with BOSSIO, V.)
'Science and the first R', *New Scientist*, 6, pp. 161–2.
'Speech development in residential nurseries', *Child Care*, 13, 3, pp. 84–8.
'The teaching of personality development in diploma courses for experienced teachers', *Sociological Review Monograph*, 2, pp. 99–111.

1960 'Early, prolonged separation and emotional maladjustment', *Journal of Child Psychology and Psychiatry*, 1, 1, pp. 37–48. (with BOSSIO, V.)
Remedial Education — An Experiment: An account of two years' work by a remedial unit for maladjusted and deprived children at the Caldecott community Caldecott Community and Department of Child Study, University of Birmingham Institute of Education. (with SUTCLIFFE, B.)
'Social learning and its measurement', *Educational Research*, 2, 3, pp. 194–206.
'Some reflections on the psychological and educational treatment of handicapped children', *Special Education*, 49, 2, pp. 17–21.

1961 'Emotional adjustment among children in care. Part 1: A firm friend "outside" ', *Child Care*, 15, 1, pp. 5–12.
'Emotional adjustment among children in care. Part 2: Practical implications', *Child Care*, 15, 2, pp. 54–8.
'The incidence of some supposedly adverse family conditions and of left-handedness in schools for maladjusted children', *British Journal of Educational Psychology*, 31, 2, pp. 183–93.
'Learning difficulties of deprived children', *Acta Psychologica*, 19, pp. 392–4.
'The long-term effects of remedial treatment: A follow-up enquiry based on a case-study approach', *Educational Research*, 4, 1, pp. 62–6.
'Remedial work with deprived and maladjusted children', *Slow Learning Child*, 8, 2, pp. 73–83.

1962 'Backwardness and underfunctioning in reading in the early stages of the junior school: The results of a recent Midland survey', *Special Education*, 51, 1, pp. 14–23.
'Child care today and tomorrow', in Northern Ireland Council of Social Service, *'The Child in the Community': A report of a conference held . . . March 1962.*

'Conditions associated with emotional maladjustment among children in care', *Educational Review*, 14, 2, pp. 112–23. (with CLIFFORD, L.)

'The educational needs of children', *Child Care*, 16, 2, pp. 49–52.

' "The happiest day of my life", as judged by junior school children; a longitudinal study', *Festschrift für* Charlotte Buhler: Gegenwartsprobleme de Entwicklungs — psychologie, pp. 104–14.

'The long-term effects of remedial education: A follow-up study', *Vita Humana*, 5, 1, pp. 10–33.

'The psychological aspects of the changing structure and needs of the family', in United Nations, *European Seminar on Social Policy in Relation to Changing Family Needs, Arnhem, 1961, Report*, Geneva, UN, 1962.

'Reading difficulties', *Times Educational Supplement*, 2437, 2 February, p. 185.

1963   'The assessment of social competence — its clinical value', in National Association for Mental Health, *Clinical Problems in Children of Primary School Age. The Proceedings of the 19th Child Guidance Inter-Clinic Conference*.

'The emotional and educational needs of handicapped children', in Association For Special Education, *Report of the 26th Biennial Conference. Growing points in Special Education*.

'The influence of schooling and sex on test and general anxiety as measured by Sarason's scales', *Journal of Child Psychology and Psychiatry*, 4, 3/4, pp. 157–65. (with COX, T.)

'The psychological aspects of the changing structure and needs of the family', *Educational Review*, 15, 2, pp. 142–55.

'The reliability and validity of the Goodenough Draw-a-man test: A pilot longitudinal study', *British Journal of Educational Psychology*, 33, 3, pp. 297–306. (with PICKUP, K.T.)

'The training of teachers for remedial work in England', *Yearbook of Education*, pp. 162–9.

1964   *The Emotional and Social Adjustment of Blind Children*, Slough, NFER.

The Emotional and Social Adjustment of Physically Handicapped Children, Slough, NFER.

'The emotional and social adjustment of blind children: A review of the literature published between 1928 and 1962', *Educational Research*, 6, 2, pp. 129–38.

'The emotional and social development of physically handicapped children: A review of the literature published between 1928 and 1962', *Educational Research*, 6, 3, pp. 207–15.

'A more preventive outlook in the whole field of child care', *Contact*, April–May.

'Some moral concepts and judgments of junior school children', *British Journal of Social and Clinical Psychology*, 3, 3, pp. 196–215. (with EDWARDS, J.B.)

1965   'Chosen ideal person, personality development and progress in school subjects; a longitudinal study', *Human Development*, 8, pp. 161–80. (with GOOCH, S.)

Deprivation and Education, Longman.

Investment in Children, Longman.

'Language difficulties among emotionally deprived children', in FRANKLIN, A.W. (Ed) *Children with Communication Problems*, Pitman Medical.

'The National Bureau for Cooperation in Child Care', *Bulletin of the British Psychological Society*, 18, 60, pp. 33–7.

'The National child development study (1958 cohort)', *Bulletin of the British Psychological Society*, 18, 60, pp. 39–44.

'Psychological changes, including character disorders, following severe cerebral injury: Diagnostic and prognostic aspects', in *Atti del Congresso Europeo de Pedopsichiatria*, 2.

'The psychological needs of handicapped children', in LORING, J. (Ed). *Teaching the Cerebral Palsied Child*, Heinemann.

'Psychology — an integral part of modern life and education', in Shotton Hall, *Do We Still Need to Work in the Dark?* Shotton Hall Publications.

'Social maturity', *Child Care*, 19, 1, 2, pp. 9–11, and 47–52.

'Teaching method and rigidity in problem solving', *British Journal of Educational Psychology*, 35, 1, pp. 50–9. (with McKENZIE, I.R.)

'Teaching the cerebral palsied child: The psychological needs of handicapped children', *Proceedings of a Study Group at Grey College, Durham, April 1965*.

1966   *Adoption — Facts and Fallacies*. Longman.

'Children's judgment of wickedness: A longitudinal pilot study.

Part I: Changes in judgment between 11 and 15 years of age.

Part II: Changes of judgment over a period and progress in school subjects', *Human Development*, 9, pp. 177–90, 191–208. (with GOOCH, S.)

'The clinical significance of standard score discrepancies between intelligence and social competence', *Human Development*, 9, 3, pp. 121–51. (with WALL, W.D.)

11,000 Seven-Year-Olds, Longman. (with BUTLER, N.R. and DAVIE, R.)

Four Years On, Longman. (with GOOCH, S.)

'Prevention of handicaps in children', *Maternal and Child Care*, 2, 17, pp. 237–42.

Social Learning and Its Measurement, Longman.

'Studying 16,000 children: A preliminary report on the National child development study', *Special Education*, 55, 2, pp. 9–12. (with BUTLER, N.R.)

1967   'Early learning and later progress', *Proceedings of the Royal Society of Health*, 60, 9, pp. 885–8.

'Follow-up of adopted children', *Journal of the Medical Women's Federation*, 43, 3, pp. 146–8.

Foster Home Care — Facts and Fallacies, Longman. (with DINNAGE, R.)

'The influence of two junior school regimes upon attainment and progress in reading', *Human Development*, 11, pp. 25–41. (with REEVES, J.K.)

'The interaction of four status variables and measured intelligence and their effect on attainments in two junior schools', *International Journal of Educational Science*, 2, October, pp. 37–46. (with GOOCH, S., and LEVY, P.)

'The National bureau for cooperation in child care', *Remedial Education*, 2, 1.

'The National Child Development Study (1958 cohort)', in Association For Special Education, *What is Special Education?* (with BUTLER, N.R.)

'The practical implications of the Bureau's research work', *British Hospital Journal and Social Service Review*, 10, February

'Research in child care; practical implications of the Bureau's programme',

British Hospital Journal, 77, 10, February, pp. 265–9.
Residential Child Care — Facts and Fallacies, Longman.
(with DINNAGE, R.)
'The role of the family in supporting the unusual child', in National Association for Maternal and Child Welfare, *Current Aspects in Maternal and Child Care*, NAMCW.

1968 'The aim and work of the National Bureau', *Institute of Health Education*, 6, 2.
'The association between Sarason's test anxiety and intelligence test performance', *International Journal of Educational Science*, 2, September, pp. 227–36. (with COX, R.)
'The association of attainment and sociometric status with reported deviant behaviour in a progressive and a traditional junior school. A pilot longitudinal study', *British Journal of Social and Clinical Psychology*, 7, 3, pp. 184–93. (with GOOCH, S.)
'Children at risk and educational deprivation', in DENNEY, A.H. *Children at Risk*, Church Information Office.
'Comprehensive assessment centres', *British Hospital Journal and Social Review*, 15 November.
'Design and aim of the NCDS', in College Of Special Education, *Research Relevant to the Education of Children with Learning Handicaps*.
'The first four years', *Mother and Child*, 39, 6, pp. 8–12.
'Pool of knowledge for people involved in child care', *Times Educational Supplement*, 1137, 22 November.

1969 *Caring for Children*, Longman.
'Caring for children', in *Growing Up in the Community*, Goldsmith College, University of London.
'Cooperation in family and child care', *British Hospital Journal*, 29 October.
A Directory of Voluntary Organizations Concerned with Children, Longman (with DAVIE, R., and HANCOCK, L.E.)
'A longitudinal study in the relationship between anxiety and streaming in a progressive and a traditional junior school', *British Journal of Educational Psychology*, 39, 2, pp. 166–73. (with LEVY, P., and GOOCH, S.)
'The National Bureau for Cooperation in Child Care: A progress report', *Bulletin of the British Psychological Society*, 22, 76, pp. 201–3.
'Planning and programming for child care', in *Selected Papers on Learning Disabilities*, San Rafael, Calif., Academic Therapy Publications.
'Policy implications of child development studies', *Concern*, 3, pp. 40–8.
'Regional difference in child behaviour', *Eugenics Society Bulletin*, 1, 4.

1970 *Able Misfits*, Longman.
'Able misfits', *New Society*, 16, 410, pp. 239–42.
'The behaviour and adjustment of seven year olds in England, Scotland and Wales: Some comparative results from the National Child Development Study. (1958 cohort)', *Scottish Educational Studies*, 2, 1, pp. 3–10.
The Challenge of Thalidomide, Longman. (with FIDDES, D.O.)
'The changing scene', *Concern*, 6, pp. 20–6.
'Cooperation in child and family care', *Concern*, 5, pp. 4–16.
Living with Handicap, Longman. (with YOUNGHUSBAND, E., BIRCHALL, D. and DAVIE, R.)

'The National bureau for cooperation in child care', in BUTCHER, H.J., and PONT, N.B. (Eds.) *Educational Research in Britain Vol. 2*, University of London Press.

'Scotland for good parents and happy children', *Times Educational Supplement*, 9 January, p. 4.

'Why are the most stable pupils found in Scotland?' *Education*, 136, 14, pp. 318, 328.

1971 *Born Illegitimate*. Slough, NFER. (with CRELLIN, E. and WEST, P.)

'The challenge of prevention', *Royal Society of Health Journal*, Congress issue, pp. 145–9.

'Community living for children — future needs of child care', in Caldecott Community, *Community Living for Children*, Ashford, Caldecott Community.

Deprivation and Education, 2nd ed., Longman. (1st ed., 1965)

'Policy implications of child development studies', *Assignment Children*, July–Sept., pp. 113–28.

'Work with disadvantaged youth in Great Britain ', in WOLINS, M., and GOTTESMAN, M. (Eds.), *Group Care*, Gordon and Breach.

1972 'Are parents necessary?' in National Children's Bureau, *The Parental Role*, NCB.

'Better adoption', *New Society*, 20, 509, 29 June, pp. 676–8.

'Born illegitimate', (Research Feedback), *Concern* 8, pp. 7–13.

'Could do better?' *Good Housekeeping*, April, pp. 91–3.

'Deprivation and education', in *Education: Annual review of the Residential Child Care Association*, 19, pp. 16–24. RCCA.

Growing Up Adopted, Slough, NFER. (with SEGLOW, J. and WEDGE, P.)

'In place of one's own', *Child Adoption*, 68, pp. 15–22. (Also reprinted in *Child Adoption: A selection of articles on adoption theory and practice*, ABAFA.)

'Language development and reading attainment of deprived children', in REID, J.R. (Ed.) *Reading Problems and Practices*, Ward Lock Educational.

'The National Children's Bureau', *Spectator*, 7503, 15 April, pp. 601–3.

'The roots of violence and vandalism', *Community Schools Gazette*, 66, 7, pp. 325–32.

(Also reprinted in *Therapeutic Education* 1, 1, 1973, pp. 3–11, and *Concern* 11, 1972–3, pp. 17–24.)

1973 *The Effects of Disadvantage on Educational Attainment*, Council for Education Advance.

'The needs of handicapped children and their families', in PALMER, J.W. (Ed.) *Special Education in the New Community Services*, Ron Jones Publications.

'The preschool comprehensives', *Where*, 81, pp. 165–7.

'Social adversity and its effect on the intelligent child's achievement', *Proceedings of the Royal Society of Medicine*, 66, 7, pp. 1203–4.

'Ten years of luck and logic at NCB', (interviewed by M. Hoffman) *Times Educational Supplement*, 3045, October, p. 14.

'Total approach to under-fives', *Times Educational Supplement*, 1 June, p. 4.

'The underachieving intelligent child', *Proceedings of the Royal Society of Medicine*, 66, 12, pp. 1201–8.

1974   *Advances in Educational Psychology 2*, University of London Press. (with Varma, V.P. Eds.)

'Born illegitimate — born at risk', *Journal of Psychosomatic Research*, 18, 4, pp. 229–33.

'Early child care in Britain', *Early Child Development and Care*, 3, 4, pp. 299–473 (whole issue). (with Naidoo, S.)

'Early prolonged separation and educational maladjustment', in Williams, P. (Ed.) *Behaviour Problems in School*, University of London Press.

'Every day two children . . .' *The Observer*, 25 August, p. 18.

'The future role of special education', *Conference Proceedings*, Council for Special Education.

'Identifying deprivation in children', *Proceedings of the Royal Society of Medicine*, 67, 10, pp. 1061–3.

The Needs of Children, Hutchinson.

'The vicious circle', in NAMCW *The Vicious Circle, 61st Annual Conference Report, 1974*.

1975   'And still we have no policy for children', *The Observer*, 13 July.

Early Child Care in Britain, Gordon and Breach.

(with Naidoo, S.)

'Early child care in Britain', *Concern*, 18, pp. 13–19. (with Naidoo, S.)

'Prevention — impossible dream or essential reality?' *Concern*, 17, pp. 26—7.

'Priorities for children', *Where*, 108, pp. 240–4.

'Seedcorn of the future', *Times Educational Supplement*, 3129, 16 May, pp. 35–36.

'Setting the scene', *Concern*, 17, pp. 6–8.

'Who is on the child's side?' *The Observer*, 19 January.

'Young children need full-time mothers', *The Listener*, 94, 2430, pp. 565–6.

1976   'Antidotes to the battering "disease" ', *Community Care*, 132, pp. 14–16.

'Discussion points on low cost day care', in *Low Cost Day Provision for the Under-Fives*, DHSS and DES.

'Familias vulnerables — ninos en peligro', in Instituto De Ciencias Del Hombre, Madrid, *La Familia, Dialogo Recuperable*.

'New thinking that makes woman's traditional role a more attractive prospect', *Times*, 13 January.

'On child abuse', *Municipal Review*, 47, 563, pp. 225–6.

'A policy for families — or for children?' *Concern*, 22, pp. 25–9.

'A policy for young children', in *Low Cost Day Provision for the Under-Fives*, DHSS and DES.

'Reducing the costs of raising children in inadequate environments', in Talbot, N.B., (Ed.) *Raising Children in Modern America: Problems and Prospective Solutions*, Boston, Mass., Little Brown and Co.

'Rights of adults or needs of children?' *Times Higher Education Supplement*, 23 July.

'The roots of violence, and vandalism', *Virginia Journal of Education*, 69, 5, pp. 17–21.

'Seebohm's children', *Municipal Review*, 47, 561, pp. 158–60, 167. (with others)

1977   'The care of young children', *Part-timer*, 8, p. 3.
        'Delinquency — a new approach', *Contemporary Review*, 231, 1343, pp. 314–8.
        'The effects of emotional and intellectual deprivation', *Proceedings of the Royal Society of Medicine*, 70, 1, pp. 24–7.
        A Future for Intermediate Treatment, PSSC. (Chairman: Dr. Pringle)
        'Giving children a chance', *Community Care*, 187, pp. 20–2. (with HOOPER, L.)
        'How early is early?' *Midwives Chronicle*, 90, October, pp. 239–41.
        'How to cut the cruelty', *Sunday Times*, 9 October.
        'In place of one's own: looking beyond research', in ABAFA *Child Adoption*.
        'Intermediate treatment: an overview', *Concern*, 24, pp. 6–11.
        'Parental deprivation in under 5s', *Proceedings of the Royal Society of Medicine*, 70, 1, pp. 24–7.
        'Whither residential child care?' *Concern*, 26, pp. 5–10.
        'Why special education?' in Joint Council for the Education of Handicapped Children, *Conference Report: International Conference 1975*, NCSE.
1978   'Beyond the backlash', *Times Educational Supplement*, 3288, 14 July, p. 2.
        'The Bureau's Development Guide 0 to 5 year-olds', *Concern*, 27, pp. 5–8.
        'The care of young children', *Contact*, June, pp. 6–7.
        'Child cruelty — what price prevention?' *Mother and Baby*, July.
        Controversial Issues in Child Development, Elek. (with PILLING, D.)
        'Fostering — the most demanding child care task', *Foster Care*, 16, pp. 10–12.
        'Giving mothering back its dignity', *Community Care*, 227, pp. 26–8.
        'International year of the child: A personal perspective on its potential', *NCSS/Briefing*, December, p. 4.
        'The needs of children (i.e., The needs of maltreated children)', in SMITH, S.M. (Ed.) *The Maltreatment of Children*, Lancaster, MTP Press.
        'A ten point plan for foster care', *Concern*, 30, pp. 5–10.
        'Towards the prediction and prevention of abuse', *Bulletin of the British Psychological Society*, 31, May, p. 185.
        'Why prevention?' *Concern*, 29, pp. 5–9.
1979   'Child deprivation in Britain', *Medikasset Magazine*, 12, 3, pp. 4, 6, 12.
        'How far have we come?' *Community Care*, 278, pp. 16–17. (Five views on present day child care — Dr. Pringle is one of the five interviewed.)
        'How to assess the way a child acts', *General Practitioner*, 8 June.
        'My Year of the Child hopes', *Municipal Review*, 49, 589, pp. 234–5.
        'Putting children first', *Concern*, 33, pp. 5–10.
        'Shared parenting', *Mother and Baby*, February, p. 52.
1980   'Aims and future direction', in PUGH, G. (Ed.) *Preparation for Parenthood*, NCB.
        'Child abuse: the uses and value of prediction in child abuse', *Safety Education*, 150, pp. 24–5.
        A Fairer Future for Children: Better Parental and Professional Care, Macmillan.
        The Needs of Children, 2nd ed., Hutchinson.
        'Opening the doors to child care', *Social Work Today*, 11, 43, pp. 16–18.

'Parenthood begins with a 'p' — for preparation, priorities, pride', *House-craft*, 53, 4, pp. 97, 99.

'Partners in the market place', *Concern*, 37, pp. 30–2.

'Sex education or preparation for parenthood', *Times*, 1 May, p. 11.

'Towards the prediction of child abuse', in FRUDE, N. (Ed.) *Psychological Approaches to Child Abuse*, Batsford.

'Towards the prevention of child abuse', in FRUDE, N. (Ed.) *Psychological Approaches to Child Abuse*, Batsford.

1981   'Needed — a policy for young children', *Early Childhood*, 1, 4, pp. 12–15.

'Preparation for parenthood', in ROGERS, R. (Comp.) *The Parliamentary Parcel for the International Year of the Child*, IYC Trust, pp. 11–12.

'Towards a caring society', *Concern*, 41, pp. 6–15.

'Towards more effective prevention of child abuse', *Concern*, 39, pp. 16–19.

1982   *Investment in Children*, Exeter, University of Exeter.

'The needs and rights of children', *Contact*, June, pp. 6–8.

1983   'The needs of children and their implications for parental and professional care', in FRANKLIN, A.W. (Ed.) *Family Matters: perspectives on the family and social policy*, Pergamon.

Index

preschools, comprehensive 16, 17, 21–6,
      148
preventive health care 17–18
preventive measures
      child care 31–2, 71, 75
      under-fives 16–17, 22
Pringle, M.K. 44, 46, 49, 78, 87, 98,
      100, 121
Prosser, H. 166
Pugh, G. 123

Recognition, *see* Praise and recognition
remedial education 55–60
Rendel, L. 51, 58
residential care 14–15, 44, 46, 67–74, 137–8
      education attainment in 69
      ethnic minority children 68
      role of 69–70
residential care staff 46–52, 72–3, 138
*Residential Child Care — Facts and
      Fallacies* 68
respite care 34–5
responsibility, need for 48, 86–7, 100,
      130–31
retarded children 54
rights
      children 114, 116–17, 150–51
      children in care 73, 80
      parental 62, 114
Ringler, N.M. *et al.* 101
Ripple, L. 64
Roberts, J. 101, 102
Rogers, D. *et al.* 93
Russia 15, 51
Rutter, M. 9, 99
      et al. 124, 170

Samaritans 118
schools, preventive role 115–16
security, need for 8, 84, 98–9, 128
Seebohm 27, 117
Seglow, J. *et al.* 120
single parents 4–5

Smith, S.M. 94
special education 87–9
special needs *see* handicapped
speech development *see* language
      development
Steele, B. 102
Strauss, P. 96, 100, 113
substitute care 9–10, 51
      co-operation in 27–42
substitute parents 3–5
      see also
            adoptive parents
            foster parents

Teachers 36, 56
therapeutic communities 48, 70
Tizard, J. 84
twins 46–7

Uncle and Aunt scheme 73
under-fives
      day care 13–19, 147–8
      deprived 46–7
      preventive measures 16–17, 22

Vandalism 127–36
violence 127–36
voluntary work 41–2
volunteers 41–2, 141
vulnerable children 28–9, 34–5, 36–7

War 146, 165–6
Wedge, P. 166
Who Cares? 73, 150
Wiberg, B. 101
wolf children 1
Wolkind, S. 101
Wooley, P. 116
working mothers 10
World Health Organization 150
Wynn, A. 113

Younghusband, Dame E. 148